CW01369869

EDWARDIAN CONSERVATISM:
Five Studies in Adaptation

Edited by
J.A. Thompson and
Arthur Mejia

CROOM HELM
London • New York • Sydney

© 1988 J.A. Thompson and Arthur Mejia
Croom Helm Ltd, Provident House, Burrell Row,
Beckenham, Kent, BR3 1AT

Croom Helm Australia, 44-50 Waterloo Road,
North Ryde, 2113, New South Wales

Published in the USA by
Croom Helm
in association with Methuen, Inc.
29 West 35th Street
New York, NY 10001

British Library Cataloguing in Publication Data

Thompson, J.A.
  Edwardian conservatism: five studies in
  adaptation.
  1. Conservatism—Great Britain—History
  —20th century.
  I. Title II. Mejia, Arthur
  350.5'2'0941   DA42

  ISBN 0-7099-4323-7

Library of Congress Cataloging-in-Publication Data

ISBN 0-7099-4323-7

Typeset by Pat and Anne Murphy, Highcliffe-on-Sea, Dorset
Printed and bound in Great Britain by
Biddles Ltd, Guildford and King's Lynn

Contents

1. Introduction   1
2. Lord Hugh Cecil: Religion and Liberty   11
   Arthur Mejia
3. Field-Marshal Earl Roberts: Army and Empire   41
   R. J. Q. Adams
4. Lord Willoughby de Broke: Radicalism and Conservatism   77
   Gregory D. Phillips
5. George Wyndham: Toryism and Imperialism   105
   J. A. Thompson
6. Lord Halsbury: Conservatism and Law   129
   Richard A. Cosgrove

Notes on Contributors   151

Index   152

1
Introduction

Conservatism is not an ideology but a frame of mind, an outlook, a general approach, grounded in temperament, psychology, economic interest, or any combination of these factors. Conservatism, therefore, takes on the colouration of time and place far more readily than such movements as Christianity or communism, which, however much they may be splintered, do owe allegiance to a common body of thought, or, at least to some extent, to a common tradition. Conservatism is thus nearly impossible to define with precision; Eugen Weber has written of the varieties of fascism,[1] but the varieties of conservatism are far more numerous.

In Europe conservatism changes, often dramatically, as one crosses national borders; from century to century, even from decade to decade, it may change within a single country. Even the broadest definition must be qualified continuously, and patterns are often difficult to discern. One of the finest treatments of modern conservatism, René Rémond's study of the French right,[2] suffers from the effort to place all modern French conservative thought in one of three traditions; at times his desire to maintain a precise historical pattern takes precedence over the chaos of reality. An additional and particularly vexing problem is the emergence of a 'new right' in the twentieth century; utterly different from the classical or traditional right, and stemming in great part from the left, it is nevertheless often confused with true conservatism.[3]

In the case of England one encounters problems caused by the resistance of the English to precise philosophical formulation. Yet it is possible to discover common denominators in British conservatism, and much writing has been done on the subject.[4] In eighteenth and early nineteenth-century England two conservative tendencies developed: the Tory and the Whig. The Tories looked to God; the Whigs looked to history. The Tories found the Whigs unprincipled; and, even if they did abandon belief in divine right, Tories continued to take a more exalted view of the monarchy and the prerogatives of the Crown. The role of the Church loomed larger in their minds. The Whigs, on the other hand, were forced by the fact that they were powerful because of a revolution to be more flexible. The eighteenth-century Whig was, in many instances, a very grand figure,[5] far less apt to be influenced by nostalgic notions of throne and altar than the Tory squire. But even this simple statement oversimplifies. As Lewis Namier has emphasised,[6] there were not Tory and Whig parties, for politics was a matter of individuals and cliques pursuing favour and patronage; moreover, even the words 'Tory' and 'Whig' were used without any attempt at precision, and well into the nineteenth century their specific political meanings were exceedingly vague.[7]

By the 1830s, however, the modern political party emerged, although its birth was difficult.[8] The 'Tories' became the conservatives, and had little ideology, which was both a strength and a weakness. Clearly the young Benjamin Disraeli saw it as a weakness, and virulently attacked Sir Robert Peel for the flexible and pragmatic tone of the Tamworth manifesto.[9] Disraeli was one of those Tories who craved ideology, and for that reason, among others, he split the Conservative Party in the 1840s over the issue of the repeal of the Corn Laws. This drove the Peelites out of the party, and so narrowed its base, largely to the landed interest, that it was doomed to minority status for a generation. Peel's dream of a party which would blend continuity and change, and which would represent all forms of property, was postponed. Yet by the 1860s Disraeli was becoming a Peelite, and managed to adjust to the world of mass politics. He became interested in party organisation; he was — to say the least — flexible in his attitudes over the Reform Bill of 1867; in his Crystal Palace speech of 1872 he largely succeeded in capturing the issues of patriotism and imperialism for the Tories. Eager for power, he exploited the dislike felt by much of the middle class for Gladstone and managed to take advantage of the vacuum left by the death of Palmerston.[10] In other words, Disraeli put ideology behind him and presided over the development of a Peelite party. Disraeli was, therefore, presiding over the merger of the Tory and the Whig strands of British conservative thought. This represented no little change for a man who, when

Introduction

young, had denounced many persons he particularly loathed as Whig, that is, as men without principle. Although there were still many prominent political figures who called themselves Whig and who did remain within the Liberal party, the conservative tradition represented by Whiggery was now at home in the Tory party, and the eighteenth-century distinction between the Tory and Whig conceptions of conservatism had largely vanished. God and history were now one.

Yet, in the middle of the nineteenth century, there were still some men who were ill at ease without ideology, and who looked upon Disraeli as Disraeli had once looked upon Peel. One of the principal antagonists of the older, flexible Disraeli was the young, rigid and principled Robert Arthur Talbot Gascoyne-Cecil, the third Marquess of Salisbury.[11] Compromise was anathema to Cecil, who believed that morality did not end at the doors of Parliament. But it was not long before the responsibilities of office mellowed Salisbury, and he was a most pragmatic Tory when he was Prime Minister; although he was primarily interested in foreign affairs, his governments did produce some striking pieces of domestic legislation, one of which, the Local Government Act of 1888, 'was a substitution of the democratic for the aristocratic principle.'[12] Even if the act can be seen as 'no more than an inevitable sequel to the Reform Act of 1884,'[13] it does show a certain relaxation on the part of the Marquess. In fact, Salisbury's hold on the Conservative Party was 'his blunt common sense and scepticism.'[14] His successor and nephew, Arthur James Balfour, also seemed to be in the tradition of the flexible Tory; Balfour, in fact, carried his flexibility to the point of feigned indolence.[15] He was a shrewd and tough political fighter, however, and, as his philosophical writings show, held firm views. But in whatever way one may judge Balfour, he was in the tradition of Peel and the later Disraeli: determined to remain in power, he was willing to compromise and waffle. He certainly regarded the Tory party as the natural and right governing party, but he understood that it must be willing to adapt to changing circumstances. Balfour had an understandable prejudice in favour of the landed interest, but he also realised that newer propertied interests must have a role in the party — even if some of them were far too vulgar for his own taste.

At the beginning of the twentieth century, therefore, it might be argued that the Tories of England were an extraordinarily realistic group of men; not without a struggle, but nevertheless decisively, they had put behind themselves the rigidities of the early Tories, and the ideological passions of the young Disraeli and the young Salisbury. The security and confidence of Great Britain, the accumulated wealth of Victorian industry, the willingness of old elites to welcome new elites, the effects of such institutions as the public schools,[16] and the traditions of an open society had all combined to produce a constitutional conservative party which played an integral role in the political process. The lack of such a conservative party, it has been argued, has been one of the disasters of modern France.[17]

But the twentieth century brought new issues and new problems, and British conservatives had a difficult time responding. Continental conservatives often cast aside their traditionalism and embraced radical, neo-Bonapartist doctrines,[18] or had often plunged into a kind of 'cultural despair.'[19] Britain had the advantage of political continuity, but nonetheless the stresses caused by national rivalries, by the birth of the Labour Party, and by the advance of political democracy were very great. The threat of economic and social democracy was thought to be real, and was seen as destructive of all the highest values of civilised society. Many conservatives were willing to be flexible within the rules of a game they knew; but in a strange world, with different standards, or with no standards at all, tolerance and fair play seemed to make little sense. As Winston Churchill later said in another context, there can be no neutrality between the fire and the fire brigade. Fair play made sense among gentlemen: was it of any relevance in the midst of criminals and barbarians? Many of the Tories of England, therefore, had serious adjustments to make. Their concerns were sensible and understandable. Even in the last quarter of the twentieth century one may well wonder if parliamentary democracy is compatible with mass democracy; parliamentary democracy, after all, was created by and for a leisured, literate, upper and upper-middle class. It was devised as a game for the few; can it be played by the many? Moreover, was it unreasonable to wonder if Britain, faced by severe challenges from ruthless and ambitious foreigners, could afford the luxury of parliamentary democracy? Just how the conservatives of England reacted is accordingly of vital importance to an understanding of modern Britain. Had a large number of them turned to authoritarianism, had more of them reacted with horror to 'the slum of democracy',[20] the history of modern Britain and modern Europe might have been profoundly different.

Introduction

The dilemma of the Tory was therefore complex. What is striking is that even the most determined and militant of them, the Diehards, those who turned against their own leadership and voted against the Parliament Bill of 1911, were often men of great resourcefulness, engaged in imaginative efforts to adapt to a changing world. They were certainly concerned with maintaining their own position in society, but they were also exceedingly worried about Britain's position in the world, and were willing to try all sorts of new expedients in order to arrest national decline and decay: 'It was their stress on novel means for preserving the old system which characterized the diehards' approach'; in fact, they anticipated the modern 'radical right.'[21] The more extreme of them could thus be described as having, to quote Lord Robert Cecil, 'a contempt for conservatism as such.'[22] Those instances make one realise that parts of the British right were not as different from their opposite numbers on the continent as is often supposed. But as a general rule British conservatives remained flexible and non-ideological; if they did cling to old values, they also could yield gracefully, and they showed skill and insight in attempts to formulate entirely new approaches to the problems of the modern world, approaches that might permit the survival of their nation and the way of life they loved.

Because of the nature of British Toryism it would be presumptuous to classify any five men as 'typical'. Nevertheless, the five men we propose to discuss *do* represent common denominators of Toryism at the beginning of the twentieth century. Their primary concerns — religion, the Army, the landed interest, the political system, and the law — are among the overlapping and passionate concerns of all British Tories. These men present varying degrees of rigidity and flexibility, of adaptation and resistance, of ideological certainty and intellectual doubt. But if no one of them is typical, their common struggle gives a picture of a traditional world attempting to adapt to modernity. None of them is ready to surrender; none of them is prepared to admit that his fundamental values are worn out and irrelevant. Yet they all understand that survival will be difficult.

Lord Salisbury's son, Lord Hugh Cecil, is a fascinating and significant figure. Best man to the radical Liberal Winston Churchill in 1908, he clung to his high Anglicanism, and lamented the encroachment within the Tory party of businessmen with their 'American' ideas. The increasing influence of Joseph Chamberlain filled him with despair, for he had an acute sense of the danger

Introduction

for the social fabric implicit in transatlantic economic and social forms. Lord Roberts was a national hero, who had achieved fame amid the tumults of the Victorian empire; much of his career strikes one as charmingly antique, something out of a nineteenth-century schoolboy novel. But in his retirement he emerged as a singularly modern man; he tried to persuade his countrymen to recognise that they lived in an age of militarism, and to face up to the consequences. His campaign for national service was a very important aspect of the pre-war decade. Willoughby de Broke gave up a great amount of the time that he would have liked to spend in his beloved Warwickshire hunting foxes, and went off to London to fight the Parliament Bill, which he was sure would wreck the constitution of England. With considerable imagination and flair he argued for the values of rural England and attempted to devise ways in which those values might be preserved in the modern world. He was not a blind reactionary, but a man who was convinced 'that Toryism, if it was to survive, must justify its existence;'[23] he hoped for a new Toryism, in which 'each man and woman will be known not by *who* they are, but by *what* they are.'[24] George Wyndham loathed the modern world, and was horrified by the appearance of men and habits of low order in his world. He urged his son never to marry an American or a Jewess, and maintained that all power was vested in the sovereign. Yet he was a man of great learning and sensitivity, and was primarily responsible for one of the most enlightened attempts to reconcile Ireland, the Land Purchase Act of 1903; his career was ruined by the revenge of its opponents. Equally fascinating is the aged and tough Lord Halsbury. Proud of his ancestry and trained in the law, he turned against much of the modern world with fury. His love of the law is comparable to the love of the land in others, and he is remembered today for the great compilation of English law that bears his name. The common law is based on pragmatism, and has always resisted intellectual rigidity; Halsbury sensed, however, that precedent must be respected, and change must be gradual, or the fabric of society will be damaged, perhaps beyond repair. Much of the history of the twentieth century underlines the accuracy of his perception.

There was a fundamental confidence about these men and their values. They

> belonged to, they led in, and they felt themselves charged with the fortunes of, a small privileged class; which for

Introduction

centuries had exercised a sort of collective kingship, and at the bottom of its thinking instinctively believed that it had a divine right to do so.

These men thought that England had become great because of the leadership of their class, 'and the function of the lower orders was limited to giving the system a popular *imprimatur* by helping to choose which of the two aristocratic parties should hold office.'[25] They honestly did not think that a parliament made up of men without the habit of rule, without the hereditary right to rule, would be capable of maintaining the greatness of their country. In the Tory tradition they continued to appeal to the electorate on their record and on their general fitness to be trusted in government, as well as by pointing out the evils of their opponents' programme.[26] Yet they also realised that the twentieth century was different, and that power was being exercised in cruder terms. More and more power was

> the ideology of their party — power to preserve power, to control movements which, if ignored or alienated, could sweep them away. From this conclusion it was a very short step indeed to the conviction that for the Conservatives to be out of power would lead to national catastrophe. This belief gave the Conservative Party a passion, a venom, a cohesion and an unscrupulousness . . .[27]

The attempt of five Conservatives to reconcile traditional values with the radical imperatives of the modern world is the theme of this book.

Notes

1. See his *Varieties of Fascism* (Van Nostrand, Princeton, N.J., 1964).
2. *The Right Wing in France from 1815 to de Gaulle*, translated from the French by James M. Laux (University of Pennsylvania, Philadelphia, 1966).
3. There is an excellent survey of modern right-wing movements in Hans Rogger and Eugen Weber (eds), *The European Right: a historical profile* (University of California Press, Berkeley and Los Angeles, 1965). In many nations men of the left, in the interest of national pride and national glory, turned against liberal democracy, and did so in the name of their own revolutionary heritage; they were often met by men of the right,

searching for a platform from which to appeal to the masses in an increasingly democratic age. For the case of France see Zeev Sternhell, 'Paul Déroulède and the origins of modern French nationalism', *Journal of Contemporary History*, 6, no. 4 (1971); Paul Seager, *The Boulanger affair* (Cornell University Press, Ithaca, 1966); Robert Soucy, *Fascism in France, the case of Maurice Barrès* (University of California Press, Berkeley and Los Angeles, 1972); and Eugen Weber, *Action Française* (Stanford University Press, Stanford, 1962); these works illustrate the confusion of 'left' and 'right' and of 'conservatism' and 'radicalism' which, with inevitable variations, appeared in all European countries. See also Ernst Nolte, *Three faces of Fascism*, translated from the German by Leila Vennewitz (Holt, Rinehart and Winston, New York, 1966), and S. J. Woolf (ed.), *European Fascism* (Random House, New York, 1968).

4. See, for instance, R. J. White, *The Conservative tradition* (N. Kaye, London, 1950), which contains an excellent statement of the Conservative outlook and 'philosophy'. See also R. B. McDowell, *British Conservatism 1832–1914* (Faber and Faber, London, 1959); Lord Butler (ed.), *The Conservatives, a history from their origins to 1965* (Allen and Unwin, London, 1977), especially Part I, Norman Gash, 'From the origins to Sir Robert Peel'; Robert Stewart, *The foundation of the Conservative Party 1830–1867* (Longman, London, 1978); Martin Pugh, *The Tories and the people 1880–1935* (Basil Blackwell, Oxford, 1985), especially Chapter 1 on 'The Conservative Dilemma'; W. H. Greenleaf, *The British political tradition*, volume 2, *The ideological heritage* (Methuen, London, 1983); and Samuel Beer, *British politics in the collectivist age* (Alfred A. Knopf, New York, 1966), Chapter 1.

5. See the classic description by Lord David Cecil in *Melbourne* (Constable, London, 1954), Prologue.

6. Especially in *The structure of politics at the accession of George III* (Macmillan, London, 1960), originally published in 1929.

7. See Norman Gash, in Lord Butler, *The Conservatives*, p. 37: 'Though the Foxite Whigs had persisted in calling Pitt's administration "Tory" because it was a creation of the King, the Pittites had never accepted that description. Only gradually was the name "Whig" successfully monopolized by the opposition; only by default did the Pittite party passively acquiesce in the label "Tory" in the years after Waterloo. But by the reign of George IV such distinctions lacked much significance other than historical.'

8. For a history of the Conservative Party see Robert Blake, *The Conservative Party from Peel to Churchill* (Eyre and Spottiswoode, London, 1970); see also the Butler, Stewart, and Beer books cited above, note 4.

9. On Disraeli see Robert Blake, *Disraeli* (Eyre and Spottiswoode, London, 1966), and Disraeli's own *Vindication of the English Constitution* (Saunders and Otley, London, 1835); important themes are developed in Paul Smith, *Disraelian Conservatism and social reform* (Routledge and Kegan Paul, London, 1967), and E. J. Feuchtwanger, *Disraeli, democracy and the Conservative Party* (Clarendon Press, Oxford, 1968). On Peel see Norman Gash, *Mr Secretary Peel* (Longman, London, 1961), and *Sir Robert Peel* (Longman, London, 1972).

10. One must not assume that Disraeli or his associates underwent a

Introduction

dramatic ideological conversion: 'The leaders of the party were generally reluctant to accede to popular demands for constitutional and other reforms and were most reluctant to accept the leaders of new social groups into the higher councils of the party. This only occurred when the pressures were very strong. The major pressures forcing the leaders of the party to accept new men, initiate reforming legislation and agree to a degree of democracy in the organization of the party, was the determination of the leaders to achieve and hold power.' Zig Layton-Henry, 'Democracy and reform in the Conservative Party', *Journal of Contemporary History*, XIII, 4 (October 1978), 653–4. Moreover, 'It could be said of Disraeli as Lord Beaverbrook wrote of Lloyd George many years later, that "he did not seem to care which way he travelled provided he was in the driver's seat."' Robert Rhodes James, *The British Revolution: British politics 1880–1939* (Methuen, London, 1977), p. 17. On Palmerston see Jasper Ridley, *Lord Palmerston* (Constable, London, 1970), and on Gladstone, Philip Magnus, *Gladstone* (J. Murray, London, 1954), and Richard Shannon, *Gladstone: 1809–1865* (London, 1982).

11. On Lord Salisbury see the biography by his daughter: Lady Gwendolen Cecil, *Life of Robert Marquis of Salisbury*, 4 volumes (Hodder and Stoughton, London, 1921–1932); see also Michael Pinto-Duschinsky, *The political thought of Lord Salisbury 1854–1868* (Constable, London, 1967) and Paul Smith, *Lord Salisbury on Politics* (University of Cambridge Press, Cambridge, 1972). It is expected that Richard Shannon's forthcoming *The rise of Tory democracy 1867–1902* will expand our understanding of Salisbury's administration.

12. R. C. K. Ensor, *England 1870–1914* (Clarendon Press, Oxford, 1936), pp. 294–5.

13. R. K. Webb, *Modern England, from the eighteenth century to the present* (Dodd, Mead, New York, 1968), p. 422. Interestingly the act does not seem to have greatly weakened, at least initially, the aristocratic role in local politics. Gregory D. Phillips, *The Diehards: aristocratic society and politics in Edwardian England* (Harvard University Press, Cambridge, Mass., 1979), Chapter 4.

14. Rhodes James, *The British Revolution*, p. 74.

15. On Balfour see Blanche E. C. Dugdale, *Arthur James Balfour*, two volumes (G. P. Putnam's Sons, New York, 1937); Kenneth Young, *Arthur James Balfour* (G. Bell and Sons, London, 1963): Alfred Gollin, *Balfour's burden* (A. Blond, London, 1965); Sydney Zebel, *Balfour, a political biography* (Cambridge University Press, Cambridge, 1973) and, most recently, Max Egremont, *Balfour: a life of Arthur James Balfour* (Collins, London, 1980). An important work which is vital to an understanding of Balfour's record as a party leader is John Ramsden, *The age of Balfour and Baldwin* (Longman, London, 1978).

16. The public schools are a particularly important aspect of the formation of the nineteenth and twentieth-century English elite. The literature on the schools is immense. Some excellent works are: Edward C. Mack, *Public schools and British opinion since 1860* (Methuen, London, 1941); J. R. de S. Honey, *Tom Brown's universe* (Millington, London, 1977), and John Chandos, *Boys together: English public schools 1800–1864* (Yale University Press, New Haven, 1984). The most important attack on the public

schools, which is also a scathing indictment of the English upper classes, is Corelli Barnett, *The collapse of British power* (Eyre Methuen, London, 1972), pp. 24–43.

17. See, for instance, Seager, *The Boulanger affair*.

18. See note 3.

19. The expression is from the title of Fritz Stern's book about aspects of the right in Imperial Germany: *The politics of cultural despair* (University of California Press, Berkeley and Los Angeles. 1961).

20. The phrase was used by Lord Esher in a letter to Lord Milner in 1917. See Maurice V. Brett and Oliver, Viscount Esher (eds), *Journals and letters of Reginald Viscount Esher* (Ivor Nicholson and Watson, London, 1934–8), IV, 80.

21. Phillips, *The Diehards*, pp. 111–12.

22. Quoted in ibid., p. 133.

23. J. R. Jones, 'England', in Rogger and Weber, *The European Right*, p. 44.

24. Quoted in Phillips, *The Diehards*, p. 156.

25. Ensor, *England 1870–1914*, p. 387. Ensor was referring specifically to Balfour and Lord Lansdowne.

26. See Ramsden, *The age of Balfour and Baldwin*, p. x. For a general picture of the 'philosophy' of Conservatism in modern Britain see H. Gleckman, 'The Toryness of British Conservatism', *Journal of British Studies*, 1 (1961), no. 1.

27. Rhodes James, *The British Revolution*, p. 17.

2
Lord Hugh Cecil: Religion and Liberty

Arthur Mejia

Lord Hugh Cecil is generally regarded as an extraordinarily bizarre figure. Although a man of great charm, he was also, it is often argued, a moral and political antique, an anachronism and a strange relic of a distant past. It must be admitted that there is considerable if superficial justification for such prejudices.

Lord Hugh was born in 1869, the youngest child of the third Marquess of Salisbury, one of the great figures of late Victorian diplomacy and politics. Lord Salisbury was also one of the leading philosophers of high Toryism, for, to him, the intellectual justification of Toryism was as important as its practical application.[1] So it was in a world of high politics and high thinking that Lord Hugh grew up, and his family's seat at Hatfield was always his spiritual home; indeed, it was for most of his life his only home, as he never had a house of his own until he became Provost of Eton in 1937.

He was clearly a strange boy. He was so unusual that his older brothers decided that he was the missing link; his nickname, always used by his family and friends, was thus 'Linky'.[2] He was 'a tall, thin fellow with a stoop', who reminded 'one of the old-time ascetic or of a High Church Curate'.[3] His voice was like 'the quacking of a sad but melodious duck'.[4] He loved controversy, seeing it, as Kenneth Rose has said, as 'one of the privileges of civilized life'.[5] After Eton (briefly) and Oxford (where he received a First in history) he eventually decided on a political, as opposed to a religious life, and in 1895 was elected MP for Greenwich.

Religion was nevertheless central to his view of life; nothing else meant anything unless it had religious belief as its foundation. Every bit as much as Gladstone he saw politics as an extension of Christianity, and he never wavered in this approach to world affairs. Often this was confusing and annoying to friends and opponents, and Oswald Mosley, however wrong he may have been in other matters, was absolutely correct when he asserted that Lord Hugh's 'religious convictions traversed and permeated his whole political being'; in fact, 'they were dragged into the most inappropriate occasions'.[6]

But of course there were, for Linky, no occasions that were inappropriate for religion. At the very beginning of his parliamentary career he made it clear what his priorities were, emphasising that there was no more momentous question that could be presented to the House of Commons than that of Christian teaching, 'because it involved the issue of national faith or national apostasy, and national apostasy . . . meant ruin'. There could obviously be no compromise on Christian issues, for

> if we preserved our national faith it mattered not in the end what catastrophes might overtake us, we should rise again from every defeat with renewed vigour and renewed power of usefulness and greatness. But if it were destroyed we should fall inevitably and never rise again.[7]

He followed this theme with remarkable consistency, and it is striking that at the very end of his parliamentary life, when he was sitting as Lord Quickswood in the House of Lords, he was making many of the same points. Speaking on D-Day, 6 June 1944, he attacked the education bill then under consideration, arguing that it gave no protection to the religious life of the people. Religious teaching would be diluted by attempts to be neutral in matters of doctrine, and he saw a widespread tendency 'to substitute the worship of man for the worship of God'. Later in the month he expressed his horror that religious instruction would be given by those who themselves did not practise religion:

> What a miserable sham the whole Bill then becomes! Are you going to say you are promoting the religious life of the nation by teaching a nominal syllabus, to which, it is perfectly clear, the teacher by his own life and example attaches not the smallest value . . . Such a pretence of religious education would be a sham indeed and a scandal from one end of the country to another.[8]

In fact, it is difficult at times to differentiate between Lord Hugh fighting for religious education in the 1890s and Lord Hugh doing the same thing in much the same way in the 1940s.

His passion, his monomania, on the subject of religion was responsible, it is asserted, for the inability of Lord Hugh to persuade others, and even to hold high office. He was made a Privy Counsellor in 1918, and his friend Winston Churchill, for whom he was best man in 1908, arranged for his barony in 1940, yet he never achieved the office many of his contemporaries thought worthy of him. In the years before the first World War he was a leader of the 'Hughligans', a ginger group of Tories who achieved a reputation for parliamentary disruption of the most extraordinary nature. The high (or low) point of their career was reached on 24 July 1911, in the fight over the Parliament Bill. Linky led a group of MPs in shouting down the Prime Minister. The next day *The Times* commented that 'to exaggerate the intensity of the passion displayed in the House of Commons would not be possible', and, although it deplored the action of Lord Hugh and his allies, admitted that the Prime Minister was performing 'unparalleled violence upon the Constitution'. Nevertheless, it did say that 'it is with great regret that we observe the prominent part which Lord Hugh Cecil took in the disorderly scene'. He had gained a reputation, *The Times* went on, for raising debate to a high level, and now that he represented a University seat, it was 'lamentable that he should prove a ringleader in Parliamentary rowdyism'.[9] Such notoriety obviously did him no good.

Yet what seemed to make him an even more arcane figure was the passion he showed for what much of the world regarded as utterly irrelevant issues. He was, in the minds of many of his friends and colleagues, lost in a kind of medieval trance. Even his obituary in *The Times* remarked that

> causes seemed to retain for him . . . something of their first romantic spell, and men in the dim, religious light of principle to be sometimes seen as causes walking. Neither humour nor friendship nor contact with various worlds of men, though all were his, served altogether to convert a born knight errant into a finished man of the world.

This obituary reiterated the theme so often repeated during his life: 'The splendour of his oratory . . . [was] as incontestable as its limitation. He could fascinate, interest, amuse, delight, inspire; yet he could not persuade.'[10] One of his most loyal supporters, his nephew Lord David Cecil, struck the same note a few years later. Lord David emphasised that Linky and his siblings were out of touch with their contemporaries, and based their lives on assumptions that were different from those of their generation. They impressed others, they were respected, 'but they didn't influence'.[11]

But even a hostile observer would, one imagines, come away from accounts of Lord Hugh with a strong admiration for the charm and humour that he and the other Cecils of his generation possessed. They were, David Cecil wrote, 'strong personalities, able and argumentative, unconventional and uncompromising, unpunctual, unaesthetic and notable for the way they contrived to combine high-spirited humour with passionate moral convictions'.[12] David Cecil tells a revealing story about an encounter he had with his uncle at the age of thirteen:

> I described someone to my Uncle Hugh as 'good'. 'What do you mean by good?' inquired my uncle. 'Someone who makes other people happy,' I suggested; it was the best I could do at thirteen. It was not enough for my uncle. 'Any capable licensed victualler can do that,' he commented. I burst out laughing; I found my Uncle Hugh immensely amusing. But I also made a mental note to the effect that I should take the trouble to think more precisely.[13]

The nephew, moreover, thought that it was a mistake that Linky's mother talked him into a political as opposed to a religious career, for he was not a man of action; he was interested in what he thought, not in getting things done.[14] Following his eccentric thoughts to their natural conclusions was what he liked. It was for these reasons that he was never thought of as a minister of state. But there was always 'in him a youthful, light-hearted, irresponsible strain which made him like young people' and made them like him. He loved to talk, it seems often just for the sake of talking; his friends understood him, and would not take offence, as strangers might, were he to burst out 'your opinion is both irrational and immoral'.[15] But those persons who did not understand could be brutal in their reaction: 'there was in his performance in Parliament a strain of almost unbridled vindictiveness, a power of vituperation which his father . . . would neither have sought nor desired to emulate'.[16] And many persons who came into contact with him found it difficult to be very sympathetic, even bishops of the Church of England. One 'was astonished at the obsoleteness of his opinions, the subtlety of his arguments, and the cast-iron rigidity of his mind. He is a medievalist in the methods of his reasoning, the strength of his prejudices, and the obscurantism of his outlook'. But at least it was admitted that 'he has an aristocratic dignity and a natural authority, which adds solemnity to words themselves never slipshod or superfluous'.[17]

One of the most charming and revealing accounts of Lord Hugh was written in September 1907 by Lady Gwendoline Bertie, shortly to marry John Churchill. She wrote to her soon-to-be brother-in-law, Winston Churchill, who the next year was to ask Linky to be his best man:

> Do you know Lord Hugh Cecil? Of course you do, & I expect he is quite a friend of yours. I have been staying in the same house as him, and he is very delightful, I liked him very much — what is so nice about him is that he is all life & spirit, and he deals so delightfully in those rapid transitions by which ones attention & ones imagination is arrested & excited. He is very instructive, never tedious; his intellect is elevated to a great height, he is wonderfully familiar with all sorts of abstract subjects, but at the same time he conciliates the pretentions of inferior minds, like my own, by dropping down to this level, in to these pursuits & ideas with a naturalness and fervour, which delights his humble listeners, and which above all, puts them at their ease, that is a great art, which only the great & clever achieve, I am sure.[18]

It is not surprising that he liked social life, taking it up particularly in the years when he was out of Parliament, from 1906 to 1910. One was always glad to see him, and if, as his nephew wrote, he was a man to whom Nietzsche and Ibsen meant little, and who remained fundamentally a contemporary of Burke and Johnson, he was none the worse or weaker for that.[19]

The question must still be answered, however, whether Lord Hugh is worth the attention of the serious historian of modern England. After all, if he is but an eccentric curiosity, then his memory can well repose in the occasional footnote or the odd anecdote. But the fact is, Lord Hugh was a serious and systematic thinker, who was attempting with considerable success to bring his views to bear on the realities of the modern world. This does not mean that he was willing to compromise those views, but he applied them to a great number of the issues of his day, often in a striking manner, and his efforts often placed him at odds with his own party and with his own friends. It is of course necessary to keep in mind his basic assumptions, but he did approach the problems of the twentieth century, not in a mood of blind reaction, but with the conviction that his beliefs were relevant to the analysis and solution of those problems.

The key to Lord Hugh's philosophy is his belief in liberty and free will. Indeed, Lord Hugh could not conceive of conservatism except in terms of religious faith. This fact permeates his book *Conservatism*, written for the Home University Library in 1912, as does the philosophy of Edmund Burke.[20] *Conservatism* is one of the major statements of the conservative case in modern England, and is his only major publication. In it he makes many of the usual points about the conservative cause, such as the need for continuity, the sanctity of private property, and the need to understand that society is an organism and not a mechanism, but he is by no means blindly Tory in his approach. The Conservative Party, he argues, by delaying for too long Catholic emancipation, the reform of Parliament and the repeal of the Corn Laws, violated Burke's principle of preventive reform. If Catholic emancipation had come earlier there would have been no agitation for Home Rule, and Ireland, under the conservative guidance of the Roman Catholic Church, would have become a steadying part of the United Kingdom.[21] The fault with Sir Robert Peel was not philosophical, but practical: he did not have sufficient foresight. And if Peel was too slow, Disraeli was too quick and 'rated too low the moral disaster that was involved in Conservatives outrunning reformers and "dishing the Whigs".'[22]

But it is soon made clear that the foundation of conservatism is religious and ethical; the importance of religion in Burke's *Reflections on the Revolution in France* is emphasised. Christian morality, he stresses, as expressed in the New Testament, is the ethical standard of the Conservative Party, and for Lord Hugh all political philosophy stems from that vital point.[23] The New Testament, for instance, says very little about the state, and it thus becomes clear the Christ was not a socialist, for socialism depends on state control. The New Testament deals with spiritual matters and with the next world, and places this world and material matters in a secondary place; it is also highly individualistic. Yet Christianity also stands for social reform: 'It cannot be denied that there is strong ground for Christians to censure the existing organization of commerce and industry. The competitive system is certainly not a Christian system.'[24] But it is clear that capitalism, even if not specifically Christian, cannot be easily replaced, for it 'requires . . . a change in human character to satisfy the Christian objection to trade and industry. Socialism does not pretend to change human nature.'[25] Self-interest will still be there, and self-denial is useless morally if done under compulsion, as would be the case under socialism. Therefore in the dangerous world of the twentieth century one returns to the basics: 'Probably no function of Conservatism is more important at the present time than to watch over the religious life of the people in the sphere of politics.' Religion is the standard by which politicians must be judged, and 'a religious purpose must purify their aims and methods'.[26]

These assumptions underlie his economic outlook. Wealth has little to do with ethics. Earned wealth is not more worthy than unearned wealth, and to distinguish between the two is wrong. Nearly everything we get is done with the help of others; 'the pecuniary value of exertions is determined by wholly non-ethical economic causes.' Lord Hugh, in fact, places virtually all economic issues beyond ethical and moral considerations. 'Taxation according to merit can seem possible only to those confused in thought.' It is 'impossible for the State equitably to distinguish between one kind of property and another'. 'If expenditure for the benefit of particular classes is to be honest, it is essential that it should be separated in the national accounts from expenditure which is in the interest of all the community . . .' There 'must be some maximum limit of the proportion of a man's property taken by taxation beyond which no tax, even in the case of the richest taxpayers, ought to go. Wanting this limit, taxation may develop into robbery.'

> Taxation only begins to invade the right of private property when either it is levied on one portion of the community in order to be spent for the benefit of another portion, or when it is so high that it cannot be reasonably distinguished from a pecuniary fine.

And, to sum up:

> Conservatism ought not to be, and at its best is not, the cause of rich people, but it ought to be the cause of the defence of property against unjust treatment. It ought to be so, not only

because property is an institution required for the sake of the common good, but also because the owners of it, like other human beings, are entitled to be guarded against undeserved injury.[27]

Much of this, of course, sounds very much the argument of any man from a rich family, with rich friends, who wishes to construct some kind of an argument to hold on to that wealth. And at times Lord Hugh does seem to be using moral arguments to argue against high taxes. Yet the fundamental point is, in the overall picture, that economics is beyond ethics and is a secondary field. Even if one of the principal aims of conservatism is the protection of wealth, it is wrong for one to say that one 'deserves' wealth even if one has earned it.[28] Lord Hugh, by putting economic issues lower than religion and ethics, brings a flexibility to economic issues that contrasts not only with socialism but also with the passions of a Joseph Chamberlain, whose views Lord Hugh disliked quite as much as those of Karl Marx. Chamberlain and Cecil both suffered from monomania, but Lord Hugh would argue that his monomania was about basic values that need a place in the modern world.

The role of the state in the modern world is also accepted by Lord Hugh, but with limits. He avoids both statism and the extemes of *laissez-faire*. The state, he grants, is of great importance, for the physical and moral environment depend on it, but the individual comes first: 'Morality is an individual matter, and this gives a primacy to the individual over the state.'[29] Toryism and socialism are not one hundred per cent opposed, for 'Modern Conservatism inherits the traditions of Toryism which are favourable to the activity and authority of the State.' The state must seek common good. But even in acting for the common good the state may not inflict injustice on an individual. As one would expect, Lord Hugh prefers voluntary action and self-help to state intervention, as they promote vigour. Workmen, for example, should combine rather than rely on the state. This line of argument gives him an excellent opportunity to preach against tariff reform, for, he maintains, protection can lead to socialism by stimulating trusts, thereby bringing about an undue concentration of power in the hands of a few men, which is just as dangerous as undue concentration of power in the hands of the government.[30]

Therefore, Tories are all for social reform, but never if it is accompanied by injustice. To alleviate poverty by taking from the rich and giving to the poor would not work in any circumstance, but more important, it would be unjust, and justice comes first.[31] Tories are also all for national greatness. National greatness is consistent with Christian teaching, but there is a moral limit. Dangers start when 'foreign policy begins to imply the lessening of another nation'. All of this is vague, he admits, but some moral guide is better than none.[32] The English constitution, he affirms, is marvellous. The monarchy has been strengthened as it has withdrawn from politics, but he does fear that too passive a monarchy might lose respect. The Parliament Bill of 1911 was, however, a disaster, for by weakening the House of Lords it weakened a vital part of the Constitution, where high rank and civil service came together. But he wants Conservatives and Liberals to play an equal part in devising a reformed House of Lords, in which the hereditary role would still play a part. And of course the Lords are necessary to check 'imprudent and revolutionary' change coming from the Commons, which needs reform itself, for 'it is the obedient instrument of whatever political party has a majority of its members'. He deplores the extreme partisanship that now characterises much of politics — an interesting observation from one of the most partisan of men — and dislikes the manner in which partisans control the state by their control of the parties. He regrets the loss of independence on the part of MPs, and sees elections as a matter of organisation and mechanism. Home Rule is appalling for many reasons, but especially because it would lead to the dissolution of the United Kingdom. At any rate, the English are the wisest people in the world, and, one assumes, Conservatives are the wisest of the wise: they support the existing social order, out of love for what is and also out of dread of injustice to individuals posed by advocates of revolutionary change.[33]

Lord Hugh never lost his interest in the theoretical bases of conservatism, and his themes never changed. After the war he wrote a political pamphlet which is a fine summary of his views. One should never apologise for being a Conservative, for conservatism is compatible with progress; it is, one gets the impression, absolutely necessary for progress. Conservatism makes progress continuous with the past, and brings the peace and security necessary for progress. Liberty is all-important for Conservatives; under socialism or communism, liberty would be impossible, for we would all be slaves of government officials. And, of course, the Church is of primary importance, for 'We are a mutually interdependent society of Christian human beings who love one another and are bound to help one another.'[34]

Of particular interest is the manner in which Lord Hugh links many of his favourite ideas by references to 'natural instinct'. For instance, property has a moral basis, for it arises from human instincts, and 'to violate the human instinct of possession is just as bad and immoral as violating the instinct against pain. In theological language it is a sin.'[35] A few years later he returned to this theme in detail, arguing that

> A man is entitled to acquire and possess because he likes to do so, and because it is the normal human instinct. And they are wrong who say there must be some element of service to justify property, or some kindred moral justification. Who would hear of such an argument in respect to life or marriage?[36]

Thus, if the state sees fit to set a limit on the amount of money one may have, soon it might set a limit on the length of one's life. Love and marriage are primary rights because they, like property, are a natural instinct. Natural instincts are part of the human personality, which itself is a divine work.

Another human instinct which Lord Hugh singles out for particular attention is the instinct of deference to some one 'exalted in station', which, as he says, is of great political and social importance. Speaking just after the death of Queen Alexandra, he commented:

> how general and how powerful is the instinct to look up to superiors merely because they are superior, and the real importance and influence of that instinct. That by itself shows that we cannot explain our social institutions on the ground of pure utility, any more than we can explain them according to the now discredited theory of contract. We certainly cannot maintain that persons in exalted station are to be respected and looked up to either because it is useful or because of any bargain or contract that it should be done. That it is done as a matter of instinct cannot be disputed . . . It is the exalted station that sets off the civic virtues of the Royal Family; and it is the human instinct of deferring and looking up to an exalted person which is the motive power at work.[37]

And Lord Hugh quotes Burke, who, when asked why he should feel the sufferings and humiliations of the King and Queen of

France, answered, 'For the plain reason because it is *natural* I should.'[38]

It is difficult for many people to reconcile Lord Hugh's passion for liberty with what appears to be a rigid and unyielding approach to religion. For example, in a religious tract which he wrote in 1935 he gave his version of what the Communion Service might have been, and he based his speculations on the Revised Service as proposed in 1928. He asserted in that pamphlet, 'For about right and wrong no compromise is possible. They are separated by a bottomless gulf and perpendicular cliffs.'[39] This sounds as if he would be the most unbending of churchmen, but he was actually arguing that Anglicans often spend far too much time worrying about trivial matters, such as whether one should fast before Communion. He also could not believe in a hell of eternal torment: 'For those who love evil the outer darkness is the best they can have. On the other hand, I cannot believe in eternal torment.'[40] On the same basis he attacked Anglo-Catholicism, which he said lacked a sense of proportion, and hence often looked 'foolish and ecclesiastical rather than wise and spiritual'. Anglo-Catholics, he thought, were too eager to introduce a degree of archaism into the ornaments and usages of the Church; it was too much like a fancy dress ball. Anglo-Catholicism should return to 'Tractarian gravity and earnestness and austerity'.[41] The advice he gave his friend Winston Churchill in 1908 is a fine summary of the Christian attitude of Lord Hugh:

> ... remember that Xtian marriage is for Xtians & cannot be counted on save for those who are Xtians. And the marriage vow must be kept altogether — you cannot merely abstain from adultery & leave loving cherishing etc etc to go by the board.[42]

It was in the field of religion, and especially religious education, that Lord Hugh established a reputation for himself in the House of Commons. In his first years there he gave some of his finest speeches, strongly defending doctrinal teaching. At other times he seemed taken up with petty issues, on which he received little support. For example, he took very seriously whether the House should adjust its hours on Ascension Day. Lord Hugh thought it was necessary to do so to allow Christians to attend divine service. It was pointed out that most MPs would not be attending church anyway, and that great inconvenience and delay of important business would be involved. Moreover, precedent was against adjournment. He was not moved, and pointed out that 'while we have an Established Church, we are more or less bound to follow the religious customs of that Church; and according to the English Church Ascension Day is a festival of the greatest magnitude'.[43] He lost.

Lord Hugh was also very agitated about the Deceased Wife's Sister's Bill. Again, it was a good opportunity to play games with parliamentary rules, which he and his then political crony and fellow 'Hughligan' Winston Churchill certainly did, to the displeasure of many MPs. Lord Hugh had consistently maintained that he was in no way prejudiced against non-Anglicans — a favourite theme of his when fighting for the teaching of Anglican doctrine in the schools — but the rights of the established Church demanded respect. In fact, if there was to be an established Church at all it was not logical to violate its principles; and to allow a man to marry his deceased wife's sister would certainly violate the rules of Christian marriage. This fundamental change was to be brought about for the advantage of 'a particular class of wealthy people who had broken the law and wished to have their characters whitewashed by Act of Parliament.' He earnestly hoped that the House 'would not set aside the mass of Christian traditions . . . in this matter, and regard the law of marriage in the same way as would the manager of the stud farm'.[44] The threat to the English family was clear, for if a maiden could hope, should her sister die, to marry her brother-in-law, an element of tension would distort a series of loving relationships. Be that as it may,

> Ever since this nation had existed, from Celtic times to the present, our country had been guided by the Christian law of marriage, and now, on a Wednesday afternoon, after only four hours' debate, they were invited to overthrow that splendid tradition of moral progress. The Christian law of marriage had built a causeway across the morass of Eastern shame and lust.[45]

The next year he was again fighting for religious marriages; after all, the relationship of the sexes is a spiritual matter, and cannot be treated from 'an animal point of view'. Moreover, 'nobody supposes that which is immoral can be made moral by Act of Parliament'. Should there really be two kinds of marriage, a church marriage and a state marriage? Should the bill pass, marriages would exist 'combining treachery and lust in a hideous degree'.[46] As was so often the case, an insufficient number of MPs agreed, although the young Winston Churchill, for a variety of reasons, did.

It must be remembered that Lord Hugh was exceedingly concerned with the ability of the established Church to survive. He fought many lonely battles to preserve clerical power. He opposed a motion to take away the legislative powers of the bishops in the Lords. Bishops were just the sort of persons who should be there, he said, because their presence is to the general benefit of the community, and because they represent educated opinion. Yet, devoted as he was to the Anglican Church, he made it clear that he was in no way concerned simply with its interests: he was interested in all religion. To that end he framed an amendment, far ahead of its time, that it was desirable that 'life Peers should be added to that House, especially those who would represent the greater religious denominations other than the Church of England'. As a result, he hoped, much Non-conformist bitterness would disappear.[47] He also had to struggle against parliamentary interference in church affairs, in the form, for example, of a Church Discipline Bill, which was introduced because of the excesses of the Ritualists. Discipline should be left to the bishops, he maintained, and moderate churchmen would not be antagonised.[48] In fact, at times the Church of England did not seem to be getting even equal treatment; as Lord Hugh pointed out, in religious teaching in industrial schools and reformatories the Roman Catholics were given separate treatment, and all other denominations — Anglicans, Non-conformists, and even Jews — were lumped together.[49] Liberty, after all, should be the right of nation's church.

It is fair to say that Lord Hugh was the leading Anglican layman of his time. He would often defer to bishops, pointing out that he spoke with humility because he was not in Holy Orders; yet it was realised that he had a greater grasp of theology and church history than practically anyone else. He was a prime mover in the establishment of the Church Assembly in 1919, of which he was exceedingly proud, and the status and role of which he set forth with clarity. The Assembly provided the Church with a considerable amount of self-government; it was a private organisation, yet one with access to the Crown. This independence was exceedingly important, because Parliament often considered church measures late at night, when MPs were tired. The press of parliamentary business was short-changing the Church, but the Church Assembly, free of Erastian taint because of its independence, gave the laity a strong voice in church affairs, and except in the case of Parliament's rejection of the Prayer Book, had worked well.[50]

Many battles were fought. Lord Hugh opposed the disestablishment of the Church of Wales. If one grants that the state should recognise religion at all, he argued, then the Anglican Church was the only church which it could recognise in Wales, which after all is not a nation itself, but a part of a larger nation. Moreover, it would be wrong to take away money from the Church in Wales and use it for secular purposes; to do so would mean that 'you are hindering the course of religion; you are fighting against light and for darkness'. And he issued a bitter warning: 'Do not let us suppose that the Parliament Act destroys the moral law of the Universe. You may be able to carry Bills through Parliament, but you cannot alter the general law which governs and punishes injustice. Be assured of that!'[51]

A far more important religious battle was that in 1927 over the revised Prayer Book, one of Lord Hugh's most important defeats. He viewed 'with absolute consternation the mischief which would be brought upon the Church of England if this measure is rejected'. The proposal would bring together moderate and reasonable people, and 'you cannot get over the fact that the Church Assembly and the Bishops and clergymen and the convocation of Canterbury and York all recommend this revision of the Prayer Book'. If one is sentimental about the old services, they will continue to be used wherever desired; and, as far as those who fear that the revised version reeks of Anglo-Catholicism, Lord Hugh insisted that the new Prayer Book was indeed Protestant — the King's oath to maintain the Protestant reformed religion was safe. He paid a moving tribute to his Church, affirming that it is 'the peacemaker of Christendom', in sympathy with all groups of Christians; it is not 'merely . . . a society for the better contradiction of the Pope'.[52]

The opposition of the Low Church, the Non-conformists and their allies, was too much. There was fear that Anglicans would lose the right to call themselves the national church, and that they would become an Anglo-Catholic sect. The proposed Prayer Book, it was alleged, would narrow the gap between the Church of England and Rome, and widen the gap between the Church of England and England itself. As one would expect, there was considerable fear of the infiltration of papal views such as transubstantiation. The Prime Minister, Stanley Baldwin, supported the bill, as did the Chamberlain brothers; Baldwin argued that although Church of England was illogical, so was England; the bill still lost, by 230 votes to 205.

The bill was introduced again the next year (1928). Lord Hugh said that although there had never been any danger of Anglo-Catholicism, changes had been made that should satisfy even the most sensitive; assurances from the bishops, and a new placement for the 'Black rubric', made it clear that the Reformation was safe. But even a most moving speech could not save the bill, and it went down to defeat. It is interesting to note that the Prime Minister and all future Tory Prime Ministers then in the House supported Lord Hugh: Baldwin, Neville Chamberlain, Winston Churchill, Anthony Eden and Harold Macmillan. Clearly, Linky might wonder if the British Parliament believed in liberty for the established Church of the land.[53]

A few years later Lord Hugh found himself in another religious dispute, which sounds frivolous to a later generation, but which he found fundamental. He brought an action against the Bishop of Liverpool, and the Dean of the Cathedral, to prevent a Unitarian from preaching in Liverpool Cathedral. Lord Hugh did not view an Anglican cathedral as a kind of public meeting-house, open to all comers. For him, a Christian cathedral was just that, endowed and elected for Christian purposes. Unitarians are not Christians, he argued, for they deny the divinity of Christ. To allow them to preach in the Cathedral was 'grave scandal', which cut 'at the very roots of law and order'. Such a scandal would certainly help Roman Catholics gain converts, and he subjected the Bishop to fervent denunciations in *The Times*.[54] The Church supported Lord Hugh, but what was important to him was the survival of the integrity of the Church, for without that integrity the modern world would sink into a materialistic and relativistic morass, with few defences left against tyranny.

As argued above, liberty was the key to Lord Hugh's outlook on life. At the very time that he was engaged in some of his most bitter political disputes — disputes which gave him a reputation as an unwavering reactionary — he was carefully working out his views on the nature and role of liberty.[55] Liberty and justice must never be confused; everyone has the right to the latter, but not the former. Yet liberty is essential to progress and to virtue, for virtue is not doing right, but choosing to do right. Wisdom can only come through liberty, thus liberty must never be given up for the expedient. Furthermore, social reforms may be dangerous if liberty is threatened: 'if we are right in supposing that humanity only makes true progress by choosing between right and wrong, we must pay a great price even for the most evidently necessary social reform which involves a diminution of liberty'. Has it helped to acquire education? Whatever the answer, a big price was paid, for parents have lost a sense of responsibility, and the child's respect for parental rights has declined. Thus poverty, unemployment, hunger, cold and so forth are not excuses for surrendering liberty.[56]

Self-discipline, accordingly, is all-important, but this does not imply discipline in a military context, which simply means subordination. In the army it may be necessary, but it is not thereby a moral virtue. The Jesuits, he asserted, have great discipline, yet they have done more harm than good. He wondered, during a period of increasing industrial unrest, if some of his Conservative friends who wanted universal inculcation of drill and obedience would want all members of trade unions to obey their leaders automatically. He strongly disagreed with men like Lord Roberts on the subject of universal military training: it should be adopted only if absolutely necessary for national defence, but it is not moral. 'Obedience is in truth a non-moral habit. It may make for good, but it may also make for evil.'[57]

Equality is another enemy of liberty. True equality has never existed and never can; look at France, with its passion for liberty — it is the most bureaucratic of nations. Look at the United States: it has banished kings and nobles, but the only result has been that plutocrats have taken their place, with less sense of public duty and with more real power. This line of argument takes him into an area which today is considered racist, but at least there is consistency. Lord Hugh argued that the lack of a sense of equality has made the British better able to deal with 'inferior' races. The British deal with an 'inferior' appropriately, by placing him in the station to which he belongs. Since common sense dictates that the black man is inferior to the white man, if you believe in human equality you must decide that the black man is no man at all and thus accord him no rights. The British, however, act justly by making appropriate allowance for the infinite range of human variations.[58]

Whatever later generations may think of this, Lord Hugh is ruthless in his passion for liberty, even if his common sense is different at times from ours. He had an exceedingly shrewd fear of the power of the state, and of the tendency of human beings to give in to expediency. No doctrine, and certainly not socialism, 'must enfeeble human nature by removing from it the discipline of liberty'.[59] Moreover, immediately after the war, and in spite of all the passions a war engenders, he defended liberty against the dangers of nationalism.[60] Lord Hugh warned that 'when a man devotes to the nation to which he belongs the highest and best that he has to give, when it becomes the greatest thing that he knows, the supreme object of his love and sacrifice, there is a perversion'.[61] Nationalism is an idolatry, a turning from Christ; therefore, if war is to be avoided, man must turn to spiritual unity. In many of his writings Lord Hugh's fear of totalitarian nationalism is very much in evidence. Patriotism, he consistently maintains, is fine, and wars may be necessary, but one must never lose one's Christian perspective; above all, the state can never be superior to conscience.

Lord Hugh Cecil's political battles were waged with these values in the forefront. He loathed Joseph Chamberlain and all he stood for: the tariff reformers were materialists, concerned not with the lasting verities of civilisation, but with crude monetary gain which was their only goal — or so Lord Hugh thought. Chamberlain was, to Linky, an 'alien immigrant' in the Tory party.[62] Understandably, some of his most bitter exchanges were with Chamberlain. In a debate over the 1902 Education Bill Lord Hugh was explicit:

> There are, indeed, two imperialisms. There is the Imperialism that wishes to see this country great and powerful because it carries Christian civilisation over the face of the globe. That is a noble and splendid ambition for our country. But there is also an imperialism which thinks of nothing but studying trade returns and considering whether we can get a little more money into the country than before. That, I think, is not the noble imperialism which we ought to support.[63]

Two years later he repeated this attack, in which he said that the Empire was a sacred trust, but that there were two imperialisms, 'the imperialism which looked only to profit, and that which had its spring in Duty'.[64] There can be little doubt, in fact, that the very thought of the Tory party falling into the hands of the Protectionists, with their concentration on the amoral concerns of economics, rather than on the claims of history and religion, was anathema to Lord Hugh. But, as one would certainly expect, he stuck to his principles and remained a devout free-trader, although he disapproved of Churchill's crossing the aisle to join the Liberals, as one should stay in one's own party and fight it out. As a result, Lord Hugh lost his seat at Greenwich in 1906.

The struggle over the Lloyd George budget and the Parliament Bill was also extraordinarily intense. He detested the political scheming of the Chancellor, and the 'reforms' proposed by the Liberals in the Parliament Bill were changes which would simply increase the power of the state and destroy the British constitution and the guarantees which it gave to British liberty. The power of the state, as exercised by the party whips, would become nearly complete: 'we will be left absolutely face to face with the despotism of a bare majority without any safeguard at all'.[65] And he posed the highly relevant question: 'Do hon. Members really think, and does the country outside really think that an Assembly which is so influenced and controlled by the party whips and by the party system is fit for the gigantic powers entrusted to it under this Bill?'[66] Yet, as indicated above, Lord Hugh was not totally against all change in the nature of the constitution. He challenged the Liberal leadership, if they were really so devoted to the will of the people, to introduce the use of the referendum, to allow some sort of proportional representation and have MPs vote by ballot.[67]

There were certainly good reasons to support the Parliament Bill, and Lord Hugh's extreme behaviour at this time is often hard to excuse. When he shouted down the Prime Minister on 24 July 1911 he was obviously going too far, and when, in a wild debate on 8 August, just three days before the Bill went through, he suggested that Asquith should be tried by the criminal law, he was approaching the ludicrous. He accused Asquith of high treason, because he was overthrowing the liberties of Parliament, and turning the royal prerogative into a partisan weapon. The proposed packing of the Lords was, 'if words have a meaning', a revolutionary proceeding, and he said that the contest over Home Rule could not be settled consitutionally. But even in the midst of the drama he repeated his suggestion about the referendum,[68] a device finally used by a much later Labour government in the dispute over whether to remain in the Common Market. Most important, he always stuck to the theme of liberty, and showed a sensible understanding of the loss of independence on the part of MPs, and of the changes in the working of the British government which were giving increasing power to non-elected and non-responsible groups. He was always willing to countenance reform, but he did not like the modern political bulldozer with which later generations are so familiar.

His extreme behaviour continued over Home Rule. As far as Lord Hugh was concerned,

> There is nothing finer in the modern political history of England than the government of Ireland by the Unionist party from 1895 to 1905. It is one of the most successful achievements of statesmanship which has been seen for a long time.

And he went on to taunt the Liberals: 'You shrink from the tribunal of the people, because you know the people will stand by the people of Ulster.' Would Manchester or Liverpool go under a Dublin Parliament? he asked. Of course they would not! So why should Belfast?[69] And the next month he attacked the extremely provocative speech made by Winston Churchill at Bradford:

> The right hon. gentleman descended to a sort of rhetoric which I always think unworthy of his really very great literary talent. It reminded me of cheap champagne — a mixture of gooseberry juice and vitriol — which sometimes has an exhilarating effect at the moment, but which proves nauseating sooner or later.[70]

But humour was not the principal goal of Linky in attacking his old friend. To force Ulster under a government it loathes would be 'one of the greatest crimes recorded in history'. It would amount to 'sheer, stark, tyranny'.[71] Indeed, Lord Hugh refused to see the legitimacy of Home Rule because he declined to accept Ireland as a nation: 'I do entreat Irishmen to cast aside this sordid, silly, and degrading dream' of Home Rule, he said early in the struggle; 'Irish nationality . . . can never be anything but shameful to themselves and dangerous to the whole Empire.' The Irish should 'feel the real pride of true citizenship in the great nation to which we and they belong'.[72] He did admit, however, that if Ulster were excluded Home Rule would not be 'fundamentally inconsistent with the principles of Liberalism . . . but if Ulster is included in the Bill it can only be carried by the apostasy of hon. Gentlemen opposite'.[73] In spite of his passion, however, even his opponents during the debates over the Parliament Bill and Home Rule had to admire his force: Lord Hugh Cecil, one wrote, 'put forward the only semblance of a philosophical theory or principle advanced from the Conservative benches in the debate'.[74] In fact, throughout the debates he continued to press for some of his pet reforms, above all, proportional representation.[75]

The war itself was not enough to blunt Lord Hugh's devotion to liberty. As discussed above, nationalism could not be allowed to override conscience. His devotion to freedom extended to a defence of conscientious objection in spite of the often virulent jingoism of wartime Britain. He made his views clear, placing them in a religious context:

> In common with a great many people of all sorts of religious opinions in this country, including a great many members of the Church of England, I feel a sense of very real uneasiness at the idea that sincerely religious people, often of the highest character, are being made to suffer because they hold opinions perverse and foolish indeed, but entirely genuine and founded upon the most deep religious convictions.

It was not a matter of having sympathy with those who did not want to fight, but it was 'wrong to force a man to do what he thinks sincerely is immoral or irreligious'.[76] Although it is wrong to punish the sincere conscientious objector, it is not wrong, Lord Hugh later argued, 'to have such a system of alternative labour as would afford a reasonable test of sincerity'. This test would be rather severe, and would not favour the scholar:

> I do not think it would be possible to give intellectual people intellectual work. It would put them in a favourable position which would excite discontent in other portions of the community, and it would not test their sincerity in any degree.[77]

An issue that came up when Parliament was considering the expansion of the franchise was whether conscientious objectors should be allowed to vote. Lord Hugh strongly thought that they should be allowed to do so; after all, they had simply taken advantage of what Parliament had offered, and had offered without attaching any penalties. They should be recognised as a valuable part of national life, 'not indeed in the correctness of their judgment, but the earnestness with which they carry it out, which is an example to all'. He later returned to the defence of the conscientious objector, commenting that 'every individual is responsible here and hereafter for what he does by his own act and his own will, whether the State commands him or whether it does not'.[78] As was so often the case, he lost.

Lord Hugh was also involved in the question of women's suffrage. Before the war he had not been so much opposed to women voting as to their presence in the Commons: 'I am opposed to women in this Chamber not merely because it would be unfitting to mix the sexes in the same assembly, but because it would change the character of the assembly altogether.'[79] He had in fact set forth his views with clarity:

> I do not believe that women are enslaved, nor do I believe there is any question of their emancipation. My views on women's rights are, I believe, thoroughly conservative, for I quite accept the teaching of St. Paul, that wives are subject to their husbands, and man is the head of the woman. These are, I know, old-fashioned views, but they do not seem to me to conflict with any reasonable proposal that women who are perfectly competent to vote should be allowed to vote, that they should be encouraged to do what is well within their powers, and should go through the dignified, the serene, and the emphatically womanly function of putting a mark on a piece of paper, and dropping it into a ballot box.[80]

When, towards the end of the war, the issue of women's suffrage was being decided, Lord Hugh supported it; there were no just reasons, he thought, for opposing it. But he doubted if it would make much difference; after all, it had not made much difference in municipal affairs. But he did oppose granting women the suffrage at a different age than men; he called it 'the most absurd proposal ever put forward'. He said that 'the Bill treats a woman's age as one might expect to see it treated in the cheapest comic papers'. Furthermore, the Bill introduces a new distinction between the sexes.[81] The next month he returned to the defence of women, arguing that the vote will give them 'that legitimate political influence that is necessary'. The vote for women is 'a reasonable act of justice', and is 'a conservative measure which is likely to allay discontent, to promote justice, and to maintain the efficiency of representative institutions in Parliament'.[82]

Lord Hugh, however, always had certain reservations about the modern suffrage, for he thought that 'Voting is not a right, voting is a public function. No one has any more right to be a voter than he has to be, let me say, a politician, or a judge, or a Prime Minister, or a Home Secretary.'[83] His logical mind disapproved of many of the facile arguments for an ever wider suffrage. 'You are fit to fight at 21 and you are fit to conduct industrial functions at 21; but it does not in the least follow that you are fit to give a vote at 21 . . .' Rather than enfranchising five million women in 1928, he urged that men and women should certainly be treated equally, but that the voting age should be 25, not 21; the House of Commons, he said, has fallen in authority after each extension of the franchise, and a Commons elected by an older electorate would carry more weight. This would preserve democracy.[84] Again, Lord Hugh lost, this time by 359 votes to 16.

In the 1920s Lord Hugh's interests were more and more centred on church affairs, and his major interventions in the Commons were in such matters as the Prayer Book controversy. But the lack of morality and the absence of a Christian sense that he detected in Lloyd George and the coalition government deeply disstressed him. He was upset at the sale of honours.[85] He found Lloyd George's economic mind 'bewildering'.[86] He attacked the government's Irish policy, deploring the willingness to attempt to impose a solution: 'I am not in favour of the Bill at all, but I believe that it would be madness to proceed with a system of local autonomy unless you can afterwards say to the Irish, You have consented to this . . .' This intervention led Joseph Devlin, the refounder of the Ancient Order of Hibernians, and the MP for the Falls division of Belfast, to remark how strange it was that a Cecil, a member of a family always associated with Conservatism and Unionism, spoke for Ireland: 'the only voice to express the Gladstonian tradition is that of a son of the late Lord Salisbury'.[87]

The core of his objections to the coalition was its lack of consistency and its expediency in all things. About six months before its fall he launched a major attack on it. He admitted that, although he had not liked it from the start, he had not engaged in active opposition because it had seemed to be the only possible government. Now, however, he had to speak out, because he was convinced that the government was destroying the country:

> They have destroyed the country in Ireland. Whoever saw a policy so calamitously unsuccessful as well as so disgracefully inconsistent? They are destroying the country, I am afraid, in India. They have jeopardised the national interests by their inconceivable bungling in the Near East. The whole of the

Versailles policy of reparations combines every possible fault, and realises no possible advantage.

The personnel of the government was also appalling. He was 'quite sure that no Prime Minister could be so bad as the present Prime Minister', and that for so long as he remained in office the condition of the country would go on getting worse and worse. Other ministers remained on to the last, 'even if it consists very little with their dignity and still less with their honour'. This last remark enraged Austen Chamberlain, who asked if it was meant that he was dishonouring himself by clinging to office; Lord Hugh replied that he meant it, 'otherwise I should not have said it'.[88]

After uttering those pleasantries Lord Hugh reached the fundamental point. He urged that we 're-unite conservatism on the basis of principles', and attacked the basic premise of the government:

> Although they believe, I daresay quite honestly, that they will defeat the Labour party by making a Coalition, not founded on principle, against the Labour party, I think the government will find in the end that there is only one way of defeating revolutionary tactics and that is by presenting an organized body of thought which is non-revolutionary. That body of thought I call Conservatism. If the government will be loyal to Conservatism, loyal indeed to any one policy of coherent thought, they will succeed.[89]

Once again, Lord Hugh felt the need to emphasise principle against expediency.

It must not be thought, however, that all of Lord Hugh's interests involved religion and the ethics of conservatism. One of his most striking interests was the formation of the Royal Air Force, a passion which grew out of his brief wartime service as a pilot. Linky as a pilot with the Royal Flying Corps seems strange, but he was an adventurous man, eager to share in the experience of so many others. He may not have been a natural pilot, but he appreciated the significance of air power for the future. He also became embroiled in an exceedingly nasty dispute between Hugh Trenchard, the first Chief of Air Staff, and the Secretary of State for Air, Lord Rothermere, the newspaper owner. Lord Hugh was a fervent supporter and admirer of Trenchard, who thought Rothermere was ignoring his professional advice. Accordingly, Trenchard resigned, and the government authorised Rothermere to accept the resignation. Linky, infuriated, intervened with his friends in the government on Trenchard's behalf. This enraged Rothermere, who insisted that he desist from this type of activity: Linky refused, and went on to attack Rothermere in the Commons. Then Rothermere resigned, but the attack was maintained, with accusations that 'amateur strategists' in the Cabinet were interfering with Trenchard's operation of the RFC. This was vigorously denied by Lloyd George. But Lord Hugh was not mollified, and commented that the Prime Minister 'really seems to care about nothing except his own retention in office — himself, personally'. Lloyd George replied that that was 'one of the most offensive suggestions it is possible to make'.[90] But whatever the merits of the dispute, an independent air force had a strong supporter, who often took a leading part in the debates on air power. He was opposed to Churchill being both the Secretary for War and the Secretary for Air. He feared that Air would always come second, and that Churchill did not fully understand the importance of air power: Churchill, he commented, 'like many Englishmen', thinks he can understand without study; Englishmen even think they can understand theology and politics without study. Many of Lord Hugh's comments were of a technical nature, and he would discuss training with professional competence. But clearly one of the appeals of the issue was his fondness for the mentality of the pilot, with his sense of superiority and his individuality. They were men who were free, and thus to be admired.[91]

In his old age Lord Hugh mellowed, but he was none the less eager to take on the occasional crusade. He still liked sweeping statements: to look after the homeless is 'an absolute obligation' for Christians.[92] As has been noted, he defended the purity of Liverpool Cathedral. Even after the second World War, he was not fearful of taking on controversy. A generation before the question of the ordination of women became an emotional and exceedingly divisive issue in the Anglican and Roman Catholic Churches, Lord Quickswood, as Lord Hugh had become, maintained that

> The Romans and (in a different way) the fundamentalist Protestants are wrong in believing that there can be an easily attained absolute test for theological truth. We are not meant to attain without effort to the apprehension of truth, but are required to grope after it and often to feel some misgiving as

to whether we have attained to it. This misgiving, however, will only be felt about secondary matters.

And the issue of women as ministers of the Church is not a secondary matter, for the Bible and the history of the Church are decisive:

> I know that I myself, if I were in church where a woman ministered the chalice, should not draw near to the altar, and at the end of the service should be deeply anxious lest the Church of England had entered in a path of apostasy and could no longer be regarded as part of the Catholic Church of Christ.

If women could conduct morning and evening services soon there would be no stopping them from the ministration of Holy Communion, and

> The Church of England would, in effect, turn its back upon the great communion of Rome and of the Eastern Churches and (what is utterly inconsistent with its history) on the ancient and undivided Church, and would come to be reckoned among those eccentric sects who have at various times in Christian history, used the ministry of woman.[93]

The last two decades of his life were calm. As his old friend Winston Churchill became one of the heroes of western civilisation, Linky retired into obscurity. Being Provost of Eton, a position with few duties, suited him. He could be amusing and charming, and maintain the standards he loved in dress and demeanour, even as German bombs fell around Windsor: air-raid shelters he thought far too fussy. This is not to say that he liked old age; it was, he told his nephew, 'the out-patients department of Purgatory'.[94] Then after 1944 he retired to Bournemouth, and lived on until 1956 in dignity, and one hopes in happiness, content and secure in his faith and bachelorhood until the end.

Lord Hugh has generally been underestimated.[95] He was sometimes too witty for his own good, and this made him appear, most inappropriately, a lightweight. He had an ability to annoy. He seemed frivolous, even on serious subjects: 'I always view university reform with the apprehension of those who see an ancient building passing into the hands of what they call a Restoration

Committee.'[96] He was not in step with the thinking of the modern world: 'The law of the universe, after all, is inequality.'[97] Politicians praised his speeches, but paid little attention, even if they were friends. Winston Churchill is typical of a great number of his colleagues in this regard; Austen Chamberlain, in a letter to George V, mentioned that Churchill proved equal to Linky in debate, 'and created much amusement when he described one of Lord Hugh's speeches as "characteristic in its brilliancy and sterile ingenuity, characteristic also of that monopoly of honesty which appears to be a family and fraternal perquisite." '[98] Again and again MPs praised his intelligence and voted against him.

Yet Lord Hugh was at least as much ahead of his time as he was behind it. As a young MP he stood beside his friend Winston Churchill and defended the rights of cadets at Sandhurst; he denied that all the cadets and servants in one company should suffer because the guilty party, an arsonist, did not come forward. Eventually Lord Hugh and Churchill were supported by Lord Roberts himself.[99] Individual rights come first. He was one of the few Englishmen of his day to show concern for the plight of blacks in South Africa; Churchill assured him in 1922 that, should Southern Rhodesia ever join South Africa, the rights of blacks would be protected.[100]

It is by no means reactionary to remind the world of dangers inherent in the growth of the power of the state; a generation after his death there is, throughout the western world, an increasing recognition of the dangers of state control. It is by no means reactionary to remind the world of the primacy of the individual. It is increasingly recognised that morality must come from the individual. Lord Hugh was never, largely because of his family background and his religious faith, seduced into Hegelian worship of the nation-state. He was right to assert only a free man can be a moral man. To be good one must choose to be good. Temperance amid prohibition is not moral; it is not even real temperance. He understood that 'Liberty consists in the power of doing what others disapprove of',[101] something which is often very difficult. His warnings were often singularly appropriate:

> We must not allow ourselves to think that the action of the State and the machinery of compulsion can be allowed permanently to take the place of that natural system of liberty by which alone human beings rise in the scale of creation, by which alone true progress is achieved.[102]

Liberty, of course, means discipline, but from the discipline of liberty comes virtue.[103]

As his obituary said, it is not 'easy to disinter even from the vast chambers of the dead a parallel for him'.[104] So here, as was not often enough the case during his life, Linky shall have the last word:

> Man, the first of animals, is also made in the image of God. As time passes, he is meant more and more to be transferred into the likeness of his Creator. And the atmosphere which he must breathe thus to grow, is the air of freedom, so that in the end he may become, like his Type, perfectly free. It is absolute liberty towards which humanity is moving; and naturally those who have gone least far upon the journey are less fit for the environment of perfection than those who have gone further.[105]

Notes

1. See Michael Pinto-Duschinsky, *The political thought of Lord Salisbury 1854–1868* (London, Constable, 1967).
2. Kenneth Rose, *The later Cecils* (London, Weidenfeld and Nicolson, 1975), p. 231.
3. 'Jehu Junior', *Vanity Fair*, 18 October 1900, p. 273. See also the Spy cartoon in the same issue.
4. According to Peter Levi this voice was inherited by his nephew Lord David Cecil, on whom he had great influence. *The Sunday Telegraph*, 5 January 1986, p. 4.
5. Kenneth Rose, *The later Cecils*, p. 231.
6. Oswald Mosley, *My life* (London, Nelson, 1968), p. 148.
7. *Parliamentary debates*, Commons, 4th series, Vol. 40, cols. 1180–1 (12 May 1896).
8. *Parliamentary debates*, Lords, 5th series, Vol. 132, cols. 59ff (21 June 1944).
9. *The Times*, 25 July 1911, pp. 8, 9. Lord Hugh, after having been defeated at Greenwich in 1906, was elected for Oxford University in 1910.
10. *The Times*, 11 December 1956, p. 13.
11. David Cecil, *The Cecils of Hatfield House* (London, Sphere Books, 1975), p. 307.
12. Ibid., p. 269.
13. Ibid., p. 280.
14. Ibid., pp. 299–300.
15. Ibid., p. 301.
16. Ewan Butler, *The Cecils* (London, Frederick Muller, 1964), p. 253.

17. Herbert Henry Henson, *Retrospect of an unimportant life* (London, Oxford University Press, 1950), III, 67, 68.
18. Randolph S. Churchill, *Winston S. Churchill* (London, Heinemann, 1969), II, Companion, Part I, p. 675.
19. See David Cecil, *The Cecils of Hatfield House*, pp. 304–5.
20. *Conservatism* (London, Williams and Norgate, n.d.).
21. Ibid., p. 67.
22. Ibid., pp. 68–71.
23. Ibid., p. 48.
24. Ibid., pp. 73–89.
25. Ibid., p. 92.
26. Ibid., pp. 116–17.
27. Ibid., pp. 121–58, *passim*.
28. Ibid., p. 121.
29. Ibid., p. 164.
30. Ibid., pp. 169ff.
31. Ibid., pp. 196ff.
32. Ibid., pp. 211ff.
33. Ibid., pp. 225–45ff.
34. Lord Hugh Cecil, *Conservative ideals* (Westminster, The National Unionist Association, n.d. [1923]), p. 16 and *passim*.
35. Ibid., p. 7.
36. Lord Hugh Cecil, *National instinct the basis of social institutions*, Barnett House papers No. 9 (London, Oxford University Press, 1926), p. 9. This is a reprint of the Sidney Ball Lecture, 25 November 1925.
37. Ibid., p. 14.
38. Ibid., p. 15.
39. *The Communion Service as it might be, together with an introduction and notes by Hugh Cecil* (London, Oxford University Press, 1935), p. 19, n. 1.
40. Ibid., p. 43.
41. Lord Hugh Cecil, *Anglo-Catholics today* (London, Philip Allan, 1934), pp. 13–18.
42. Quoted in Randolph S. Churchill, *Winston S. Churchill*, II, 272.
43. *Parliamentary debates*, Commons, 4th series, Vol. 83, col. 1023 (23 May 1900).
44. Ibid., Vol. 92, cols. 1234, 1237 (24 April 1901).
45. Ibid., col. 1238.
46. Ibid., Vol. 102, cols. 475–82 (5 February 1902). See ibid., 5th series, Vol. 142, col. 2242 (10 June 1921) for a discussion by Lord Hugh of a bill designed to regularise the religious status of a man who married his brother's widow.
47. Ibid., 4th series, Vol. 67, cols. 152–4 (21 February 1899).
48. Ibid., Vol. 71, cols. 275–6 (10 May 1899). See also ibid., Vol. 69, cols. 836ff (11 April 1899) for a discussion by Lord Hugh of the proposed censure of the High-Church English Church Union.
49. Ibid., Vol. 64, cols. 185ff (4 August 1898).
50. See Lord Hugh Cecil, *The Church and the realm* (Westminster, Church Electorate Committee, 1932).
51. *Parliamentary debates*, Commons, 5th series, Vol. 54, cols. 66ff (16 June 1913); Vol. 38, col. 1310 (16 May 1912); Vol. 62, col. 1821 (19 May 1914).

52. Ibid., Vol. 211, cols. 2578ff (15 December 1927).
53. Ibid., Vol. 218, cols. 1220ff (14 June 1928).
54. See Dr L. P. Jacks *et al.*, *Two letters . . . concerning the action of Lord Hugh Cecil against Liverpool Cathedral* (London, Oxford University Press, 1934), and *The Times*, especially 23 December 1933, p. 13, and 9 January 1934, p. 12.
55. See Lord Hugh Cecil, *Liberty and authority* (London, Edward Arnold, 1910).
56. Ibid., pp. 36–8.
57. Ibid., pp. 45–50.
58. Ibid., pp. 54–61.
59. Ibid., p. 64.
60. See Lord Hugh Cecil, *Nationalism and Catholicism* (London, Macmillan, 1919).
61. Ibid., p. 42.
62. J. L. Garvin and J. Amery, *The life of Joseph Chamberlain* (London, Macmillan, 1932–69), VI, 815.
63. *Parliamentary debates*, Commons, 4th series, Vol. 107, col. 849 (6 May 1902).
64. Ibid., Vol. 129, col. 836 (9 February 1904).
65. Ibid., 5th series, Vol. 23, col. 2080 (4 April 1911).
66. Ibid., col. 2115.
67. Ibid., Vol. 25, cols. 937–8 (8 May 1911).
68. For this debate see Ibid., Vol. 29, cols. 967ff.
69. Ibid., Vol. 58, cols. 207, 210 (11 February 1914).
70. Ibid., Vol. 59, cols. 2311–2 (19 March 1914).
71. Ibid., Vol. 60, cols. 1070–1 (31 March 1914).
72. Ibid., Vol. 37, col. 93 (15 April 1912).
73. Ibid., Vol. 42, col. 592 (10 October 1912).
74. John M. Robertson, MP, *The common sense of Home Rule* (London, P. S. King and Son, 1911), p. 9.
75. *Parliamentary debates*, Commons, 5th series, Vol. 63, col. 813 (15 June 1914).
76. Ibid., Vol. 82, cols. 1055 (11 May 1916), 1570 (15 May 1916).
77. Ibid., Vol. 86, col. 823 (19 October 1916).
78. Ibid., Vol. 95, cols. 315ff (26 June 1917), Vol. 99, col. 1217 (21 November 1917).
79. Ibid., Vol. 25, col. 815 (5 May 1911).
80. Ibid., Vol. 19, cols. 106–7 (11 July 1910).
81. Ibid., Vol. 93, cols. 2189–90 (22 May 1917).
82. Ibid., Vol. 94, cols. 1655ff (19 June 1917).
83. Ibid., Vol. 249, col. 1723 (16 March 1931).
84. Ibid., Vol. 216, cols. 251–5 (18 April 1928).
85. Ibid., Vol. 116, col. 1358 (28 May 1919).
86. Ibid., Vol. 125, col. 466 (13 February 1920).
87. Ibid., Vol. 136, cols. 846–8 (16 December 1920).
88. Ibid., Vol. 152, cols. 2380–2 (5 April 1922).
89. Ibid., cols. 2388–884 (5 April 1922).
90. Ibid., Vol. 105, col. 1321 (29 April 1918).
91. Ibid., Vol. 113, cols. 1541ff (13 March 1919), Vol. 126, cols. 1610ff (11 March 1920).

92. *The Times*, 5 October 1933, p. 8.
93. Lord Quickswood, *The ministry of women in statutory services* (London, SPCK, 1951), pp. 7, 14.
94. David Cecil, *The Cecils of Hatfield House*, pp. 303–4.
95. A notable recent exception is W. H. Greenleaf, *The British political tradition*, Volume 2, *The ideological heritage* (London, Methuen, 1983), pp. 287–95.
96. *Parliamentary debates*, Commons, 5th series, Vol. 165, col. 1847 (22 June 1923).
97. Ibid., Vol. 186, col. 2483 (23 July 1925).
98. Martin Gilbert, *Winston S. Churchill* (London, Heinemann, 1977), IV, Companion, Part III, p. 1793, 3 March 1922. No grudge was held. Lord Hugh, the year before, wrote to Churchill, on the occasion of Lady Randolph's death, that 'in spite of much disagreement & disapproval I shall always love you'. Ibid., p. 1535. And, as mentioned above, Churchill arranged for Linky's peerage in 1940.
99. See Randolph S. Churchill, *Winston S. Churchill*, II, 45ff. See also the Companion to this volume, Part I, pp. 150ff.
100. Martin Gilbert, *Winston S. Churchill*, IV, Companion, Part 3, p. 1877.
101. Lord Hugh Cecil, *Liberty and authority*, p. 25.
102. Ibid., p. 44.
103. Ibid., p. 22.
104. *The Times*, 11 December 1956, p. 13. Another obituary, in the *Eton College Chronicle* for 7 February 1957, No. 3109, says that his departure 'diminished the public stock of harmless pleasure'. It is worth adding that Lord Hugh was not averse to pleasure; see, for an account of his indolent and self-indulgent life while out of parliament, John Jolliffe, *Raymond Asquith, Life and Letters* (London, Collins, 1980), p. 159.
105. Lord Hugh Cecil, *Liberty and authority*, p. 16.

3
Field-Marshal Earl Roberts: Army and Empire

R. J. Q. Adams

On 19 November 1914, Great Britain briefly put aside the excitement and anxieties of the World War in order to honour the memory of the most distinguished soldier of a remarkable age. The King-Emperor attended at St Paul's Cathedral to mourn his most decorated subject; five field-marshals, five generals and two admirals bore the coffin to its final resting-place. Ironically, Frederick Sleigh, Earl Roberts of Kandahar, was buried close to the grave of Field-Marshal Lord Wolseley, his oldest rival, in the great crypt dominated by the tombs of Nelson and Wellington — the place where Britain buries her most honoured soldiers and sailors. Those who were there agreed that it was a fine and fitting ceremony. So loved was he that those who had served under him wondered whether there was any suitable way in which his king and country could properly celebrate the memory of the 'little field-marshal', known to them as 'Bobs Bahadur' — Bobs the Brave.

Certainly he had not wanted for honours in his lifetime. He was a Knight of the Bath and of the Orders of St Patrick, St Michael and St George, the Indian Empire and the Star of India; remarkably he was the only soldier of his era to be created a Knight of the Garter. He was a peer of the realm and one of the original laureates of the Order of Merit. The breast of his tunic was covered with campaign medals, including the most prized of battlefield decorations, the Victoria Cross. He held honorary degrees from the great universities, the freedoms of innumerable cities and honorary colonelcies of more regiments than any serving officer in the history of the British Army. It can fairly be said of him that he was the greatest of the Empire's colonial guardians and, of all commanders of his time, the most beloved of the officers and men who served under him. Of the many military heroes raised up by the 'little wars' of the last century, none led a life quite so close to the stuff of which the legends of heroes are made. It was a life which can never be repeated, for it belonged alone to that era and tells as much of it as it does of him.

Roberts, like many who live long lives in dangerous professions, was somewhat superstitious and believed that things beyond human reason often affected the outcome of events. He might well have, for more than once it seemed he owed his very life to what serious historians sometimes choose to overlook — sheer luck. Yet beyond that, there were several realities, several forces which if not supernatural, were surely to play significant roles in shaping his life from beginning to end. He was born in Cawnpore, India on 30 September 1832, the son of Colonel Abraham Roberts. Herein are revealed the two most potent of these forces: the Empire and the Army.

Roberts spent little more than a decade of his adult life in England. He was in the truest sense a citizen of the British Empire — a son of the Anglo-Irish Protestant ascendancy, a paladin of the British Raj for four decades and a commander of armies on three continents. British imperialism — carried out with responsibility and under the precepts of the Christian tradition — was for him an absolute good, a force for transferring civilisation to those who were without it. Quaint as the notion seems in modern times, to Lord Roberts it was not that the acquisition and maintenance of colonies made Britain great; rather, they were the proof of her greatness. The conservation and protection of that Empire became his life's work. His faith in the rightness of this cause never flagged, and as its greatest warrior his reputation outshone even his most glorious rivals.

The other significant factor which gave meaning to his life was the Army — first the Army of the Honourable East India Company, and latterly the British Army itself. He was born the son of an officer of the Indian Army, the *de facto* rulers of much of the sub-continent. Dashing the hopes of his parents (who would have preferred for him a career at the bar), young Fred never expressed any desire other than to follow his father's footsteps into soldiering. To Roberts, the Army stood between Britain's rivals — jealous and at all times dangerous — and the nation and empire. Though he knew it to be underfunded and insufficiently appreciated, the Army was to this man who served it for sixty years the strong right arm of all the virtues of the British way of life and its civilising mission to the world. Throughout his life he advanced its cause and sought to nurture and protect it from its foreign enemies and internal critics.

Unlike most of the other subjects of these essays, Roberts was a man of action, not of philosophies. Like Burke himself, Roberts believed that a nation's history made her what she was; and these two remarkable figures would have agreed also that the best definition of patriotism was the simplest — the striving to prolong the national life in the face of all threats, within and without. For 'Bobs Bahadur', the two finest historical products of the British state — and British patriotism — were her Empire and her Army.

The child of his father's second wife, young Fred and his mother and seven brothers and sisters were settled in 1834 into a modest establishment in Ireland while Colonel Roberts returned to his regiment in the subcontinent. A sickly childhood left him stunted and weakened and blind in one eye.[1] He recovered his health as he grew older, though he was never to grow large or robust — he never stood over five feet two inches in height nor weighed much more than nine stone.

After spending his thirteenth year at Eton — and thereby overstraining the family budget — Fred's longing for the army life overcame the objections of his parents, who removed him to the Royal Military Academy at Sandhurst. The young cadet's dreams of a Queen's commission, however, were dashed two years later when Colonel Roberts arranged for his son's transfer to the academy maintained by the East India Company at Addiscombe, near Croydon. Commissions in the regulars were usually gained by purchase in those days before the Cardwell reforms, and it was nearly impossible for young officers to live on their army pay. The elder Roberts knew well that the Queen's officers treated their opposite numbers in the Indian Army as inferior stock bred in a less desirable stable. No one was more aware than he that promotion came slowly, and the very highest ranks of command — even in India — were often closed to Indian Army officers. He knew also, however, that the Addiscombe course was more brief and less expensive than that of Sandhurst, that the cost of living in India was radically less than at home and that a commission in the Indian service would allow his son to be self-supporting within a year. The issue was settled, and it was the Indian Army for young Fred.

Roberts passed out of Addiscombe at the end of 1851, ninth in a class of forty and richer by £50 and a gold watch — gifts from the proud Colonel. Within eight weeks of receiving his commission as a lieutenant of artillery, he was on a Peninsular and Orient steamer, bound for Calcutta and a connection with the subcontinent which was to last forty-one years.

Bobs, as his Addiscombe mates called him, strode into an India most unlike that of today or, for that matter, the India of post-Mutiny days. The writ of the British Crown held sway only in the most abstract sense, and actual rule was shared by the Honourable East India Company represented by the Governor-General, and several hundred greater or lesser princes, maharajas and amirs. For the purposes of making the will of 'John Company' known and for civil order and defence, the whole of India was broken down into three so-called presidencies — Bombay, Madras and Bengal — each with its own army, all under the collective authority of a commander-in chief in Calcutta. Roberts's first posting was in Bengal.[2]

Unlike regular officers, Indian Army lieutenants were as likely as not seeking a paying career. Many came from the middle classes, and, unlike the regulars, few sons of the rich and powerful made their way through the ranks of the Indian Army. A commission meant virtually a life of exile, with only one non-medical leave home during a career on the edge of empire. Promotion was customarily by strict seniority and slow in coming; and the elder Roberts, for example, did not finally become a brigadier until well past his sixtieth birthday. Pay was poor, yet the costs of luxuries were so shockingly low that there was never a shortage of young men (and women) willing to endure the heat and the distance from home for a career (or marriage) in the military or civilian service of the East India Company.

One exception to simple dogged longevity as a means to promotion was for a young officer to distinguish himself in staff work; the other more common path open to the ambitious was more exciting and required gaining distinction on the field of battle (being 'mentioned in despatches' was the phrase of the day). Hence, they did anything to get into action and, once in, displayed feats of courage which today seem insanely foolhardy. Defying death and collecting medals became a kind of cult among young men of Roberts's generation. Though 'braver officers never led men into battle',[3] the inevitable result was that many died young. Those who survived, as a hostile bullet went astray or a shell misfired, claimed the rewards for their mates. Of the forty young men who graduated from Addiscombe with Bobs, all but a handful died in action before the age of thirty. But for blind luck, on more than one occasion Roberts would have joined them.

His first station was at Peshawar, where he served as aide to his father — whose failing health required his retirement to Ireland within the year. Roberts soon earned appointment to the prestigious Bengal Horse Artillery, whose yellow jackets and polished brass helmets had attracted him from the first. Less excitingly but perhaps more significantly, he was appointed in 1856 as Acting Deputy Assistant Quartermaster-General.

Staff work within the British and Indian armies was exceedingly primitive at this time; there was no general staff, no separate intelligence branch, no advanced staff college and no strategic planning organisation. While a nightmare by modern standards, it was a splendid opportunity for an ambitious young man to make himself indispensable. Initially denied this first staff appointment because he had not mastered the Hindustani language, he learned it in a matter of months and thereafter combined his regimental duties with his new responsibilities. He could not have chosen better, as the Quartermaster-General's branch served most commanders as the equivalent of a field staff, taking charge of planning and intelligence as well as the more mundane duties of supply and training. Bobs was on his way to making himself master of the brain of his army.

Yet even this would have been slow progress without distinction on the field of battle, and his opportunity came in 1857 with the bloody and tangled episode of the Sepoy Mutiny. Largely confined to Bengal, the Mutiny was a rebellion of native mercenary troops — the sepoys — against their British officers and not in any modern sense a popular political revolt against imperial authority. The overwhelming majority of the native population and most of the rulers of the Indian states remained loyal (or neutral) to the Raj. The threat was a very real one, however, for at the time of the uprising, native soldiers in the Company's Army outnumbered Europeans by more than seven to one: approximately 257,000 to 34,000.[4]

The causes of the grisly affair are many and complicated, but all authorities agree that the immediate fuse which set off the explosion was the adoption of a new rifle. Its paper cartridge, ripped open with the teeth before loading, was rumoured to be greased with animal fat both from cows, sacred to Hindus, and swine, anathema to Muslims. True or not, many sepoys believed the stories and made ready to rebel against the sahibs who committed such sacrilege. On 10 May 1857 Indian units rose against the British at Meerhut, and the style of the conflict was set. Atrocity of the most terrible kind by the rebels — committed as likely as not against women and children — was avenged with savagery by the Loyalists. Claimed among the victims of the Mutiny were the formerly easy relationships between Indians and British; fatally wounded too was the autonomy enjoyed by the Honourable East India Company.[5]

The northern province of the Punjab was the centre of the Mutiny, and its capital city, Delhi, had fallen into the hands of the rebels. There were but 16,000 British troops of all ranks in the district, as against 65,000 sepoys. At Peshawar, Roberts joined a 'movable column', under the command of Colonel Neville Chamberlain (who was not related to the later Prime Minister), made up of all available men, to move against the capital. Throughout the summer, with its enervating heat and drought, siege was laid until the city fell in September.

Roberts was in the thick of the fighting and received his first wound from a bullet which clearly would have severed his spine but for a cartridge case which blocked its entry into the flesh. It was not the last time that chance intervened to save the young officer's life, and the legend of the 'Roberts luck' was born. In his eyes, however, the pain of the injury was a modest price to be paid for the fact that notice of his gallantry was taken. He had at last been 'mentioned in despatches'.

Roberts's adventures were not at an end, however. In late October he cheated death once again, during the siege against the city of his birth, Cawnpore, as a bullet aimed at him struck his rearing horse instead. Early in the new year, at Kudaganj, his greatest moment as a subaltern occurred: virtually unarmed, Bobs recaptured the regimental battle standard from two well-armed rebels. Again, one fired at him from close range, but the sepoy's musket misfired. For his trouble, Roberts was awarded the Victoria Cross, the nation's highest decoration for military valour.[6]

By spring the Mutiny was over, and the greatest threat to India of the entire century was past. His health seriously endangered by the strains of his campaign, Roberts was granted fifteen months' medical leave, and he set sail for Ireland in late May. In his kit he had £500 prize money and his Victoria Cross citation. More importantly for his career, his name had appeared in despatches no less than seven times — more than any other junior officer in the campaign — and he had been promised a brevet promotion to the local rank of Major upon his return.[7] Recognition of his genius for the craft of war was now assured. By June 1859, his health restored and with a new bride, the former Nora Bews (who was to be his wife for fifty-five years), Bobs again set sail for India.

Save for infrequent action in the field, including attachment to the celebrated expedition under Sir Robert Napier against the mad King Tewodros of Abyssinia,[8] Roberts's energies and ambitions were invested for the next twenty years in the QMG Department — and he was well on his way to being recognised as the resident organisational genius of the Indian Army. His appointment rose from Assistant to Deputy and finally, in 1872, to Quartermaster-General. His substantive rank rose to that of Colonel, while he attained the brevet rank of Major-General in 1875 at the remarkably youthful age of forty-two. He also began to command an impressive collection of letters after his name as he gained his first official honour, a CB, in 1872. Equally important to the successful young officer was that he and Nora were at last successful in beginning a family, as three children were born to them in the decade of the 1870s: his only son, Freddie, would follow his father into the Army and toward a Victoria Cross of his own.

Roberts's long apprenticeship for field command was to end in 1878, as relations between the Imperial Government in India and the Amirate of Afghanistan soured in the decade before that year. Since the days of the Mutiny, debate had raged within British India over how best to ensure the safety of its northern frontier. During most of this period the 'masterly inactivity' school held sway, postulating that Afghanistan was beyond the northern perimeter of Indian security.

In 1874, the Conservative Party returned to power, bringing with it Benjamin Disraeli and his imperialist enthusiasms. With the Tories came a new Viceroy, Lord Lytton, who took up the rival or 'forward' school of defence thinking, which taught that India could not achieve security against Russian ambitions without *de facto* control over the regime in Kabul. From his influential post as QMG, Roberts energetically supported this view. The year 1877 saw the outbreak of war between Russia and Turkey, leading eventually toward Disraeli's finest hour at the Congress of Berlin. It also saw a worsening of relations on the North-west Frontier, as Russia redoubled her efforts to draw the Afghans into her orbit.

By September 1878 war appeared inevitable, and Roberts was commanded to organise a new column, the Kurram Field Force, of 6,600 men and officers. Joining them were two other units under the command, respectively, of Roberts's oldest friend, General Sir Donald Stewart, and Sir Sam Browne (the inventor of the celebrated triangular sword-belt).

The British assault began on 21 November 1878. Within six months the Amir had fled to Russia, and his son and successor sued for peace. By midsummer, Bobs was recalled to summer headquarters at Simla and given a knighthood; it appeared that the long-awaited leave in Britain of which he and Nora had dreamed for years was at last a certainty. As it turned out, his work was far from done — and the groundwork of what was to become the Bobs legend was not yet complete.

On 3 September the newly appointed British emissary to Kabul, the fancifully named son of a French father and an Irish mother, Major Pierre Louis Napoleon Cavagnari, was slaughtered in Kabul, along with his bodyguard. Roberts was immediately ordered to return to his troops, now renamed the Kabul Field Force, bearing instructions from the Viceroy to take the Afghan capital any way he chose and exact punishment for the awful murder: 'It is not justice in the ordinary sense, but retribution that you have to administer on reaching Kabul.'[9] It was a strong draught for the young general. Roberts had not a cruel bone in his body; he could bear neither the sight of nor the responsibility for corporal punishment. Under martial law he would tolerate capital punishment only when evidence was overwhelming, and now he was ordered to punish to the utmost both a government and a people.

On 30 September — his forty-seventh birthday — he began his advance at the head of 7,000 men, and within six days Kabul was his. Roberts hanged the ringleaders of the mob which had murdered the British agent and his men and razed the fortress of Kabul, the Bala Hissar, while the remainder of the city went unmolested. On 13 October the news reached him of yet another reward, as he had been gazetted brevet Lieutenant-General.

Roberts considered this second phase of the war the final curtain, and again he dreamed of the more tangible prizes which awaited him. Anticipating his long overdue leave, he packed Nora and the children off for Britain and planned to join them in a few months' time.[10] By May 1880 Bobs had given over command to Sir Donald Stewart, but Lord Lytton, on the eve of his supersession by Lord

Ripon, advised Bobs to remain a bit longer in Kabul. It turned out to be sovereign advice, for within weeks the greatest of the little general's Asian adventures was to begin.

While the 'Roberts luck' was justifiably famous in the Indian Army, Bobs was not foolish enough to presume opportunity could always be depended upon to fall to him. As it happened, by July the small British garrison in the city of Kandahar, 300 miles to the south, was besieged by a much larger irregular Afghan army. Seeing an opportunity to be seized, with Stewart's permission, Roberts wrote a 'personal and secret' memorandum to the Imperial Government in Simla, in which he called for the reversal of the order to return to India and the immediate despatch of a column to Kandahar.[11] As commander he audaciously nominated himself. Rather than a rebuke for his 'pushfulness', he received full consent from the new Viceroy, Lord Ripon, to proceed.

While Bobs himself always counted the victory at Kabul as the greater accomplishment, the 320-mile march to Kandahar captured the public fancy at home far more completely than any of Roberts's other exploits. Well it might, for the trek was a 23-day nightmare through unfriendly and rugged country, in a climate which offered freezing night temperatures contrasted with 100-degree heat at midday, all to relieve a beleaguered garrison under assault by a murderous heathen horde. It was the stuff of which Victorian legends were made. While he withheld the worst details from his letters home, he made clear that the greatness of his opportunity compensated for the strain on mind and body. He wrote to his wife on 19 August:

> It would never have done for me to have been out of the way now, for this march will be one of the most memorable things of the War, and if Ayub [the Afghan leader] will only wait for us at Kandahar, it will enable me to finish the business off properly. When I have done that, then go home I must and will. . . .[12]

On 1 September the Battle of Kandahar was engaged, and Roberts lost but 35 dead and 213 wounded, compared with Afghan losses of more than 1,000 killed.[13] The Afghan–Indian frontier was again secure.

Word of the victory spread quickly, and Roberts became the man of the hour. His letterbag swelled with congratulations, including personal communications from the Queen and the Commander-in-Chief of the British Army, the Duke of Cambridge. He was notified that he would receive a GCB, and a special medal commemorating the march was to be struck — which was awarded to all participants, including his horse, Vonolel! Within a week, Roberts, now almost fifty, had been granted medical leave to return home for the first time in almost twelve years. When he boarded ship for Britain he was dangerously thin, wracked by fever and exhaustion and suffering from 'constant nausea, violent headache, pain in the back and sleeplessness with a total lack of appetite.'[14] He was also arguably the happiest man in India. He had long dreamed of returning home a conquering hero. Now, as victor at Kabul and Kandahar, he felt sure he would at last receive the glittering prizes which had so far eluded him.

Roberts's return proved to be more triumphal in appearance than in reality. He was fêted by society and showered with honorary university degrees and the freedoms of cities, but he was ultimately disappointed in the tangible rewards which came his way. The chief source of his problems was that he had incurred the wrath of the radical wing of the Liberal Party, who had returned to power the previous spring under W. E. Gladstone. Most Liberals opposed the 'forward' policy in India, and Bobs was its most staunch defender. Roberts's role as conquering hero irritated the pacifist 'Little Englanders' among the radical party, who unjustly accused him of committing atrocities in his Afghan campaign. They also hated Bobs due to the fact that his cause was enthusiastically taken up by many imperialist Conservatives, to whom his victories and his Indian policies were meat and drink.

Even worse in the eyes of many Liberals was that Roberts's new-found fame made him a rival of their own darling, General Sir Garnet Wolseley — who, it should be noted, bore the Liberal embrace only for its usefulness to his own ends.[15] Bobs was everything Wolseley was not: he was Indian Army, Wolseley was a Queen's officer; he had opposed the short-service provisions of Lord Cardwell's army reforms passed under the last Gladstone government, Wolseley had championed them.[16] Each had won popular victories and great public acclaim, but at least at this point of his career, Roberts was an Indian hero while Wolseley would forever be linked with Africa.

The rivalry between the two generals extended beyond mere popular reputations. Younger officers attached themselves to the causes of one or the other of the two champions, and the years from 1880 to 1900 saw a naked battle for power and preferment between the two 'rings': Wolseley's 'Africans' and Roberts's 'Indians'. It is ironic that each of the men sought to modernise and reform the Army and that they had every reason to co-operate. Yet they were self-made men of middle-class origins and had neither wealth nor great families behind them. The ultimate prizes — the greatest being the succession to the Commander-in-Chief, the reactionary George, Duke of Cambridge — were so few in number, however, that it was too much to hope that these ambitious men and their equally ambitious supporters could conceive of making common cause.

Roberts, then, was the Tories' man, like it or not — as Wolseley was the Liberals' — and the Liberals were in power. For his exploits in the Zulu War and at Tel-el-Kebir, Wolseley was promoted full general, given a peerage and voted £25,000 by Parliament. Roberts, for his more substantial campaign on the Northwest Frontier, received £12,500 and a baronetcy, with neither the promotion nor the peerage he so much wanted. Wolseley got the glamorous opportunity to relieve 'Chinese' Gordon in the Sudan, a mission which failed yet led to a viscountcy and, later, the command of the forces in Ireland — and, by implication, the succession to the Duke of Cambridge. Bobs was packed off back to India and the command of the Army of the Madras Presidency.[17] As Wolseley's star rose, he became in the popular mind 'our only general', Sir William Gilbert's mildly disguised 'modern majorgeneral'. To his own admirers and in the Tory press, Bobs was 'our only other general'.

Roberts's years in the Madras command were happy and largely uneventful ones. He began those reforms for which he was to become famous in later years — improving training and particularly marksmanship, as well as adding more lustre to his reputation as a soldiers' general by campaigning for higher pay for 'Tommies' and paying close attention to the living and working conditions of the men under his command, British and Indian alike.

In 1885, as the tour of duty as Commander-in-Chief in India of his old friend Sir Donald Stewart drew to a close, Bobs contemplated retirement, as the Liberal administration was not likely to second him to the command. In 1884 he had chanced to make the acquaintance of Lord Randolph Churchill, the rising star of the Conservative Party, who was touring the subcontinent at the time. Each of the men had admired the career of the other, and it was a case of friendship and common respect at first sight. Without warning, in mid-1885 Gladstone's government fell, a victim of the Grand Old Man's conversion to Irish Home Rule. A general election brought the Tories, under Lord Salisbury, back into power with none other than Lord Randolph at the India Office. Before the end of the summer, Roberts succeeded Sir Donald Stewart as Commander-in Chief of the Indian Army.

Save for a brief campaign in the jungles of Burma which resulted in the overthrow of the infamous King Thibaw, Roberts's years as C.-in-C. were profitably spent in improving the training, equipment, preparedness and conditions of life of the Army in India. His road as a reformer was made smoother by his good relations with the two viceroys under whom he served, Lord Dufferin and Lord Lansdowne — in the latter case, the general and the statesman would enjoy even more significant co-operation in future.

In 1893 Sir George White succeeded the newly created Baron Roberts of Kandahar in the India command as Bobs declined a second extension of his term. Rejecting the governorships of Malta and Gibraltar, Roberts seemed to be within sight of the end of his long career, as there were no available appointments suitable to one of his rank.[18] For the two years which followed, Roberts spent his only term on the half-pay list. With the Liberals once again in power, he settled down to a continuous round of speeches, honours and travel. At the suggestion of his friend Lansdowne he began his memoirs, *Forty-one years in India*, and completed a series of lengthy newspaper articles on the career of the Duke of Wellington.[19] While he had often considered himself rather 'buried' in the subcontinent, as Wolseley's better-publicised commands had gained him a great public following, it was during this period that Roberts realised how popular he had become. This new notoriety was enhanced by the popular poems and ballads of a young Anglo-Indian journalist, Rudyard Kipling, whose adulatory barrack-room dialect poem 'Bobs' was set to a popular tune and became the music-hall sensation of 1893.

The year 1895 witnessed the dissolution of the old soldier's fears of retirement, for he was appointed Field-Marshal (a rank which had no mandatory retirement age) in May. In June Lord Rosebery's short-lived Liberal Government gave way to the last Conservative administration of Salisbury, with Bob's old friend Lord Lansdowne at the War Office. It was a time of changes for the Army: the aged Duke of Cambridge gave up his command after thirty-nine years of resistance to change, and Wolseley, being senior to Roberts, replaced him.[20] This left the Irish command open for Bobs, and he took it up in October. He was sixty-three years of age and would live almost another twenty years, yet this brief lull between appointments was to be virtually his only real retirement.

Roberts's four years at the Curragh, near Dublin, were an unqualified pleasure — he loved the country and the people, and he continued with his army reform ideas as in India. He had not long to enjoy it, however, as by the spring of 1899 British attentions turned from Ireland and her Home Rule struggles to South Africa, as tensions between the Dutch-speaking 'Boers' of the Transvaal and Orange Free State and the government of the British Cape Colony reached the breaking point. It is not necessary in this essay to examine those differences; suffice it to say that neither Boer nor Briton wished to share authority over the Cape with the other. In October, war was declared. Roberts, aged sixty-seven and considered by many the best tactician then on active service, was also thought to be too old for the rigours of campaign. General Sir Redvers Buller was sent out to command British forces — among them young Freddie Roberts, a subaltern in the 60th Rifles — in what was thought to be yet another short colonial war which would be over by Christmas.

The Afrikaner republics, while small and underpopulated, resolved not to be trodden upon like Afghanistan or the Sudan. Rich with their diamonds and gold, well-equipped by Mauser and Krupp and absolutely dedicated to their cause, the Boers made a formidable enemy. Within two months of the outbreak of war, the British position appeared all but hopeless as the Cape Colony cities of Kimberley, Mafeking and Ladysmith were besieged, and all attempts to break the sieges failed. The second week of December — always recalled as 'Black Week' — was doomed to be recalled as the nadir of British hopes as it encompassed defeats at Stormberg, Magersfontein and Colenso.

Such disasters were too much for Roberts. The Wolseleyites had always criticised Bobs as an 'advertiser', army jargon for an officer relentless at making his own talents known to his superiors (a remarkable charge in light of the self-promotion of their champion). It is undeniable that Roberts had been an ambitious man, but now he was at an age and rank where ambition had ceased to matter. As he had done in India before the Battle of Kabul years before, he turned a blind eye to protocol and wrote directly and in confidence to his political chief, in this case his old friend Lord Lansdowne. On 8 December 1899 he wrote that success in the war 'depends almost entirely on the confidence of the Commander in being able to bring it to a successful conclusion.'[21] Roberts was convinced that Buller simply could not win the war, and he continued to his friend:

> I feel the greatest possible hesitation and dislike to expressing my opinion thus plainly, and nothing but the gravity of the situation and the strongest sense of duty would induce me to do so, or to offer — as I do now — to place my services at the disposal of the Government.
>
> The difficulty of making this offer is greatly increased by the fact that, if it is accepted, I must necessarily be placed in supreme command, and to those who do not know me I may lay myself open to misconceptions. But the country cannot afford to run any avoidable risk of failure.

This was an audacious act which might simply have earned Roberts a quick rebuke. Followed as it was by the disasters of 'Black Week', however, on the 16th — the day following the defeat at Colenso — Lansdowne ordered him at once to London. A second telegram informed him that his son had been seriously wounded in action. He crossed immediately to the capital and accepted Lansdowne's offer of the supreme command in South Africa. It was also the War Secretary's tragic duty to inform the old Field-Marshal that his son had died of his wounds. It was small comfort to the grieving father to learn that his son was to receive the first posthumously awarded Victoria Cross. Despite his crushing sense of loss, within a week he had collected a staff and set sail aboard the *Dunnotar Castle* for his new command. On 10 January 1900 he arrived in Cape Town.

Roberts's plan to reverse Britain's poor fortune in the war went contrary to that of the War Office: rather than move from Cape Town directly to the north-east toward Bloemfontein, the capital of the Orange Free State, he meant to relieve Kimberley, to the west of Bloemfontein, and then march to the east. This he did, beginning on 6 February. Here, leading the largest army he was ever to command — more than 37,000 men — he won the first significant victory of the war, raising the siege of Kimberley on 14 February and releasing the beleaguered Sir George White (and among others the impatient Cecil Rhodes). He met and defeated

General Piet Cronje at Pardeberg on 18 February, accepting the surrender of more than 4,000 Boers nine days later. This success was made more joyful by the news that Buller at last relieved Ladysmith on 1 March.

With the speed typical of his campaigns, he fought and won the Battle of Poplar Grove on 7 March[22] and entered Bloemfontein six days later.[23] Coming as quickly as it did after his arrival in South Africa and after such a shocking series of defeats, this was perhaps the high point of Roberts's military career. While much more war lay ahead, it was now clear that victory would come to Great Britain — it was only a matter of time.

After a six-week delay owing to the need for supplies to catch up with his army, Bobs set off northward in early May and on 1 June entered Johannesburg. Barely allowing time to catch their breath, Roberts pushed his men the additional dozen miles north to take the capital, Pretoria, three days later. In all, his force had marched 300 miles in thirty-four days — a feat which exceeded even the remarkable Kabul-to-Kandahar march of twenty years earlier. To all appearances, the Boer War was close to its conclusion.

There was, in fact only one more set-piece battle to be fought — that at Bergendal Farm, east of Pretoria, on 27 August — and again Roberts carried the day. Within a week, he declared the Transvaal annexed. While this was the end of formal war, it was not the end of hostilities. The Boer armies dissolved into irregular commando units, and the conflict evolved into a bitterly fought guerrilla war which would not end for eighteen more months. In late September, however, there was little tangible resistance from the Boers, who had withdrawn north to collect their forces and their wits. Roberts held the entire railway system of the Cape; 12,000 Boers were prisoners of war; even more had been released on condition that they took an oath of neutrality; there were no longer any organised Boer armies of appreciable size in the field. With this in mind, on 17 September Roberts telegraphed to the War Office for permission to lay down his command and return home.

Upon receipt of this message Lord Lansdowne advised the Government of the need to retire the prematurely aged Wolseley and replace him with Roberts; though displeased that the command had been denied to her favourite son, the Duke of Connaught, the Queen acquiesced.[24] In early December, Roberts handed over his command and the 'mopping up' to Kitchener, and embarked for Britain and the highest command in the British Army.

He was welcomed home to a jubilation which amazed him. He was received at Osborne House by the Queen, who bestowed on him both an earldom and the blue ribbon of the Garter — in the latter case, the first such honour granted to a military commander since Wellington's time. Not to be outdone, Parliament voted him £100,000 in gratitude. It must have seemed ironic to the man who recalled how unappreciated he felt by 'official' London after his victories in the Second Afghan War. The crowds loved him then, but now their admiration knew no bounds; he was truly the greatest public figure in a country with no shortage of heroes.

Lord Roberts's tenure in his new office was neither particularly happy nor peaceful, and the reasons were several. In the first place, the nation — and particularly believers in the Empire — had been shocked by the South African War, which did not officially end, it should be recalled, until 1902. The conflict cost the nation £200 million; she had placed into the field more than 400,000 men (most of them short-service volunteers) and suffered 22,000 deaths. No one saw the need for military reform more than Roberts, who was appalled at the poor preparation of the War Office.

The Government, headed after July 1902 by Salisbury's nephew, Arthur James Balfour, had no choice but to respond to this need. The great cost of the recent conflict, however, put the public in no fit mood to tolerate increased army estimates. Several royal commissions were appointed to advise the Cabinet on defence matters, while at the same time, Balfour's two successive War Secretaries, St John Brodrick and (after September 1903) H. O. Arnold-Forster, pursued their own plans. While these statesmen competed to 'save' the Army, the Commander-in-Chief had his own notions of how best to improve the service. The result was a textbook case of too many good intentions collectively accomplishing little, and substantive organisational reform was left to R. B. Haldane, War Secretary in the Liberal Government which took power in December 1905.

Roberts felt frustrated and unconsulted by his political masters; his relations with Brodrick were strained and they were little better with Arnold-Forster. For almost a decade there had been consensus on the front benches that the time had come to do away with the office of Commander-in-Chief and to replace it with a general staff along the lines of those of the other Great Powers. Upon the recommendation of a Royal Commission chaired by Lord Esher, the first step in this direction was taken as Bobs was unceremoniously retired in February 1904, and the first Commander of the General Staff (later the Imperial General Staff), Sir Neville Lyttleton, took his place at the War Office. Surrounded by any number of other crises, Balfour's government did not get around to the creation of the rest of the Staff, and that task also was left to Haldane.

The three years Bobs spent as Commander-in-Chief were not, however, without issue. Edward M. Spiers has written that, under Roberts:

> The primary focus of army reform . . . was the improved professional training of officers and men. He accepted that this focus should reflect the altered circumstance of the modern battlefield. With closed formations at an end, he maintained that future training should promote the ability of the private soldier to think and act for himself. It should also require that junior officers accept an ever-increasing amount of responsibility.[25]

He did not overlook the importance of modernising the tools of war and the manner in which soldiers were taught to use them. He prided himself on improving the standard rifle, quick-firing artillery, ambulance and store wagons, barracks and traction engines. He also began inquiries into the improvement of uniforms, infantry drill, the training of cadets at Sandhurst and Woolwich, organisation of mounted infantry, canteen arrangements and the lessening of regimental expenses.[26]

He had for years warmly supported the need for the creation of a modern general staff and was aggrieved only at the abrupt way it was put into place. As always, however, Roberts concealed his disappointment and accepted Balfour's invitation to serve as the only salaried member of the new Committee of Imperial Defence. Despite his injured feelings, he wrote to Ian Hamilton that he overcame his inclination to reject the offer because of the 'feeling that it would keep me in touch with the Army . . .'[27]

Lord Roberts was seventy-one years of age and had recently completed fifty-two years of active service. Widely acknowledged to be the nation's greatest living soldier, he had become a peer of the realm and a wealthy and greatly loved public figure who had never publicly taken a controversial position on any purely political issue and probably never cast an electoral ballot in his life. There was every reason to believe that he would live out his life in comfort and finally, as old heroes were expected to do, fade away.

Such an assumption, however, overlooked the fact that the old field-marshal took up yet another cause — an issue which would thrust him into the midst of one of the most divisive political struggles of the Edwardian years. In some ways, these would be the most tumultuous years in a life long dedicated to battle.

It is a common theme in these essays that circumstances in the Edwardian years so moved some conservatives (most but not all of whom also considered themselves Conservatives) that they felt themselves driven to pursue policies and methods which seemed decidedly unconservative: some embraced a kind of political extremism which, in others, they might have condemned out of hand as dangerous, even revolutionary. Roberts, unlike Lord Hugh Cecil or George Wyndham or Lord Halsbury, had no experience in politics or at the bar; he knew even less of the House of Lords than Lord Willoughby de Broke. Yet in the last decade of his life he joined them, and others, in attempting to sway matters of high politics. And like them, he did not shrink from positions which were unpopular and postures which his new-found critics called unconstitutional and even un-English.[28]

While he would be accused by his opponents of machiavellian motives for thrusting himself into the Edwardian political debate over defence questions, Lord Roberts's reasons were really quite transparent. There was no line of demarcation in his mind between military and political concerns. In a rare speech in the House of Lords, he explained his conception of the awesome responsibility rightly born by public men: 'we are links in a living chain,' he said, 'pledged to transmit intact to posterity the glorious heritage we have received from those who have gone before us in this place.'[29] The freedom and prosperity enjoyed by British subjects had come to those who enjoyed them only because others in earlier times had secured them. To Bobs, the greatest of benefits enjoyed by his fellow Britons was their independence from the rule of others. Ultimately, it was not her wealth or her empire which kept Britain free of outside interference — it was her Army and Navy. In the last decade of his long life he became convinced that the time had come to make sacrifices to protect the inheritance received from 'those who have gone before us', in order that it might be passed along to the next generation. Ultimately, this was his uncomplicated definition of conservatism.

The old field-marshal was not alone in his feeling that the new century held unknown dangers for Britain, for the shocking experience of the Boer War had left defence enthusiasts with the fear that the nation's military capacity was terribly inadequate. Many questions plagued them: why was the nation so unprepared? Why was the victory so long in coming? How would the nation perform in case of war with a European power; and, in that case, was it prepared to repel any and all attempts at invasion? Perhaps worst of all: what terrible lessons about Britain's national fibre and vitality were to be learned from this nasty little war?

Many informed citizens (inside and outside Whitehall) chose in the early years of the century to speculate on questions of war and strategy and the attendant wonders of military technology. For some it created a new patriotism, a latter-day 'jingoism'; for others, however, it aroused a new dread — an exciting fear of a bigger and closer war.[30]

Beginning in 1903, for example, an old form of popular literature was revived as publishers found a ready market for sensational invasion novels. After the publication in 1903 of the still-thrilling tale by Erskine Childers, *The riddle of the sands*, the genre degenerated quickly, both in literary quality and originality. The most popular of these yarns was probably William Le Queux's *The invasion of 1910*, published three years later.[31] Bobs had advised Le Queux on the verisimilitude of the book, and bound into every copy was a facsimile letter signed by Roberts himself appealing to the reader 'for the sake of all they hold dear', to take up the cause of military preparedness.[32]

These books (and their many imitators) differed from the invasion fiction of the previous century in several ways: in the first place, the proposed enemy was not France, as had been customary, but Germany — a youthful, vigorous and aggressive empire.[33] Second, the reader's attention was directed less to German perfidy than toward British decadence. Finally, these works should not be confused with anti-war literature meant simply to frighten the reader into a pacific posture: on the contrary, they were imbued with a kind of gilt-edged morality: to risk the nation's birthright through weakness was the highest treachery. Zara Steiner has observed: 'All these books shared a common assumption that war was a splendid thing . . . a glorious spectacle fought with means which far out-paced the crude imaginings of their forefathers.'[34]

Ridiculous as it might seem to historians who know the kind of war which came in 1914, to many Edwardians the idea that Britain was vulnerable to a cross-Channel invasion became a 'national obsession'.[35] To these men and women it was clear that *someone* had to do *something*. Many of them supported the formation of para-military youth organisations — the most famous of which, of course, was Baden-Powell's Boy Scouts; many read the tracts of the various bands of 'efficiency' enthusiasts; others joined the Navy League, or the National Service League or other such military-related pressure groups. Though she was devoid of any militarist tradition similar to the German or even the French example, Britain did experience a peculiar sort of popular militarism in the years between the Boer War and the first World War.[36] Into this climate of opinion Britain's greatest living soldier, an aged political novice with no powerful political party behind him, emerged to demand that the nation fundamentally alter the way in which her armies had been raised for centuries.

Lord Roberts's South African experience and his time at the War Office had convinced him that Britain was far more vulnerable than either her people or her leaders realised. Most of all he doubted that Britain maintained an army of adequate size to protect nation and empire in the event of war among the Great Powers. The Army was small and professionalised and intended primarily for internal security and garrisoning the Empire. To make matters worse, throughout the previous century army commanders had despaired over their inability to overcome the problem of insufficient enlistments. Even the greatest of Victorian war secretaries, Viscount Cardwell, had been unable to discover an answer to the constant need of the Army for sufficient numbers of physically fit men.[37]

The Boer War had required the raising of more troops than at any time since the Crimean conflict half a century earlier and revealed both the depth and potential for damage of the manpower problem. Unprepared for a land war even on such a limited scale, the War Office had turned to the only expedient available to them — a massive recruiting campaign, fuelled by wartime patriotism, to supplement the Regular Army. Roberts had not forgotten the experience of turning around a losing campaign in the field while being responsible for the training of thousands of unprepared volunteers into an army. It was a sobering lesson for which he blamed his political masters.

Not the least of Roberts's worries was the discovery, soon after he assumed command in 1900, that there remained only 17,000 regular troops in the home islands.[38] For centuries home defence had been the first responsibility of the British Navy — and the absolute reliance on the superiority of the senior service was the cornerstone of the 'Blue Water' school of defence thinking. What haunted Bobs for the rest of his life was the possibility of a general war among the Great Powers occurring simultaneously with or soon after such a demanding colonial struggle. With the fleet at sea, he reasoned, might not a Britain denuded of her regulars be defenceless in case of invasion? Furthermore, he had begun to conclude that an ambitious and aggressive Germany might be tempted to take advantage of Britain's reliance on her fleet at the expense of adequate home-defence forces.

In 1903, the Committee of Imperial Defence quietly conducted an inquiry into the question of Britain's vulnerability to surprise invasion — the so-called 'bolt from the blue' by a force small enough to avoid detection by the fleet but large enough to carry out serious operations.[39] The findings of the inquiry, made public by Balfour in 1905, assured Parliament and the nation that there was no danger from invasion, even in the absence of the fleet. It was concluded that in that event, mines and submarines would stave off any invasion force until the power of the fleet could be brought to bear.[40]

Disappointed with the findings of the CID, Bobs took his concerns before the public.[41] In January 1905 he published an article in *The Nineteenth Century* calling for the raising of a home-defence force adequate to protect the nation in the absence of the regulars. In August, before the controversy from his essay had died down, he addressed the same issue in a speech to the London Chamber of Commerce. He suggested the possibility of a major war on the North-west Frontier involving a Great Power, which conceivably could require even more troops than the recent Boer War. How then, he asked, would Britain raise them? Furthermore, how would the security of the nation be guaranteed while every possible man was away at the front and the Navy dispersed patrolling the sea lanes? Only, he concluded, the mandatory military training of all able-bodied young men could meet all these needs. With this public declaration, Lord Roberts began a campaign to bring political and public opinion around to a viewpoint which had not received serious attention in many decades: the conscription campaign which was to occupy him for the remainder of his life had begun.

In November 1905, after a final attempt at going through proper channels to convince the CID to recommend a programme of mandatory training,[42] he resigned from that body and accepted the presidency of the little-known National Service League, thereby making himself the major advocate of compulsory service in a nation which for generations had raised her armies through free enlistment.[43] He became, then, the object of hatred of all who opposed the idea of compulsory service as anti-democratic, militaristic and un-English.

Founded in 1902, the League was an obscure assemblage of peers and retired generals until Roberts took its helm. His reputation gave to the organisation a legitimacy it did not otherwise enjoy. By 1907 it had grown to more than 10,000 members; by 1909 to more than 32,000; by 1910 to 62,000, and by the eve of the World War it claimed 270,000 adherents.[44] The secret of the League's growth was not only Roberts's popularity but also his revision of their stated goals.

The NSL had been founded to press for the implementation of general conscription as practised in France or Germany; to Roberts such a plan was unacceptable, and he had so informed the members when he addressed them at their initial meeting and on the first two occasions when they had offered him their presidency. He had made his opinion clear in his January article in *The Nineteenth Century*:

> Compulsory service is, I believe, as distasteful to the nation as it is incompatible with the conditions of an Army such as ours, which, even in peace time, has always such a large proportion of its units in foreign service. I hold, moreover, that the man who voluntarily serves his country is more to be relied upon as a good fighting soldier than he who is compelled to bear arms.

Thus severing himself from the politically unpopular goal of the most extreme conscriptionists, Roberts explained that the future of the nation depended not only upon the enlisting of regular soldiers but also upon the willingness of British men 'to undergo such a modicum of training as will make them useful as soldiers when called upon by their county for personal service.'[45]

This was the goal which he forced on the League: not continental conscription but mandatory training and organisation of all young men into a home defence militia which would also serve as a pool of volunteers for overseas duty in time of war. His plan, of course, was to prevent another manpower crisis such as that during the first eighteen months of the South African War, when the nation was required both to raise and train a large force while her battlefield fortunes hung in the balance. This remained League policy until the Great War.

Not long after Roberts's death, the Conservative publicist and political 'insider' F. S. Oliver wrote of him:

> If I were asked to name Lord Roberts' highest intellectual quality I should say unhesitatingly that it was his instinct. And if I were asked to name his highest moral quality I should say, also unhesitatingly, that it was the unshakeable confidence with which he trusted his instinct . . . What gave him his strength in counsel, as in the field, was the simple modesty of his confidence.[46]

In 1905 it appeared that Roberts's confidence in his instinct had surely misled him. After accepting the presidency of the NSL, he was chided by Lord Rosebery, the former Liberal premier, for taking up a cause doomed from the outset by the electorate's refusal even to consider the possibility of any variety of mandatory service.[47] Bobs, however, was convinced that, having expunged continental conscription from the platform of the League, he could convince both electors and politicians of the need for some measure of compulsory training for home defence. Bound to neither of the great parties, he cared little which finally brought in a mandatory service bill. Given the climate of opinion in each party, however, most conscriptionists looked to the Tories for help. It was true that in these years a growing number of prominent Tories joined the League,[48] but the refusal of the party leadership to adopt NSL policy drove Bobs to exclaim to a supporter several years later: 'Please don't speak as if the National Service League were a Unionist body. It was formed in 1902 when the Unionists were in power, and they are as much to blame as the Liberals that we are still without a National Army.'[49] At least until 1909, he continued to hope that mandatory service could be achieved through co-operation between the parties.[50]

With the advent in December 1905 of the new Liberal Government led by Sir Henry Campbell-Bannerman (and after 1908 by Herbert Henry Asquith), there came to the War Office Richard Burdon Haldane. A chancery lawyer without military experience, Haldane produced a remarkable plan of army reform, including a proposal to raise a so-called Territorial Force as a second line for home defence. Following his non-partisan philosophy, Roberts and the NSL saw this as a useful, if incomplete, vehicle to achieve their ends and warmly supported Haldane's proposal in the hope that he could be convinced to add compulsory training to his scheme.[51] An attempt was made to amend Haldane's plan by grafting mandatory service on to his Territorial Force — the bill offered by one of the few Liberal MPs who belonged to the NSL, Thomas Kincaid-Smith — and it was soundly defeated on its first reading amid derisive cheers from the Liberal benches.[52] The Liberals, recommitted to the Gladstonian virtues of peace, retrenchment, reform and free trade, would have nothing to do with any kind of compulsion. Roberts and the League, therefore, were left to rely on persuasion to influence the people and Parliament to swing the Government around to their view. It was a daunting prospect, and for the remainder of his life the aged warrior was the greatest champion of the cause.

While the imposition of some form of mandatory service was supported by many individuals and identifiable groups for many different reasons,[53] for Roberts the question resolved itself to a matter of home defence. He was particularly concerned about what were to him the aggressive and dangerous foreign-policy designs of Imperial Germany. This had caused him to raise the invasion issue in 1903 and 1905, and to aid in the publication of Le Queux's *Invasion of 1910*. This was the major argument employed by the NSL in its attempts to amend the Haldane army reforms. Thwarted in these efforts, Roberts and the League raised the invasion question once again in 1907. Better prepared than in his previous attempts, Roberts led a self-proclaimed 'Committee of Four' consisting of himself, Lord Lovat, the military correspondent of *The Times* (Charles à Court Repington) and the Conservative MP Sir Samuel Scott.[54]

Motivated more by his desire to discomfit the Liberal Government than by any conversion regarding the invasion question or the need for mandatory service, Arthur Balfour in July 1907 agreed to bring the issue to the attention of the CID. Aided by information supplied from many sources — among them the former Commander of the Channel Fleet, Admiral Lord Charles Beresford, and the Commandant of the Army Staff College, General Sir Henry Wilson — Roberts and his colleagues placed their arguments before a 'blue ribbon' CID subcommittee chaired by Herbert Henry Asquith. After more than five months of hearings, quite predictably the committee dismissed as unrealistic the League argument that Britain was vulnerable to a German 'bolt from the blue' invasion by up to 150,000 men, as the full committee had in 1903 rejected the threat of a French incursion of 70,000 men.[55]

Haldane and Asquith, who became premier in April 1908, were not likely to allow findings friendly to the League. Yet public opinion in these years was regularly excited and alarmed by events which encouraged Roberts and his followers to redouble their efforts. The year 1908, of course, also saw the beginning of the political strife over *Dreadnought* building, cresting but not fully dispersing in the next year with the 'we want eight — we won't wait' movement. The autumn brought another war scare as Austria and Russia fell out over the annexation by Vienna of the Balkan sanjaks. This crisis peaked in October — the same month as the Kaiser's provocative interview with *The Daily Telegraph*. The troublesome year ended with yet another Franco-German crisis over Morocco. Michael Howard has written of the climate of opinion of this period:

> The following year — 1909, the year of the great dreadnought scare — Lord Curzon joined in the call for compulsory national service to guard against invasion which, if successful, would result in 'the crumbling and collapse of society itself . . . the utter subversion of the old order of things to which we are accustomed'; and in the Commons the Secretary of State for War was asked to comment on the rumour 'that there are, in a cellar within a quarter of a mile of Charing Cross, 50,000 stands of Mauser rifles and 7½ million Mauser cartridges.' The grave calculations of the Committee of Imperial Defence thus took place against a background of xenophobic paranoia which does much to explain the enthusiasm — almost the relief — with which the outbreak of war appears to have been so widely greeted in 1914.[56]

Hoping that the electorate — and their representatives in Parliament — were more receptive to the idea of mandatory service before it was too late, in May 1909 Roberts and Lord Newton placed before the House of Lords a bill to require a mandatory four months' training in the Territorial Force for young men reaching the age of eighteen. The field-marshal, despite his aversion to party politics, wrote to Balfour soliciting support for the measure a month before its introduction. He was mistaken, of course, for the Tory leader — like the Liberals — feared the reaction of the voters against any party which took up even the mildest form of conscription.[57] The bill was killed on its second reading. It was true that there was much covert support within the highest ranks of the army[58] and among the Conservative benches for some sort of mandatory training, and even a few Liberals (Lloyd George and Churchill among them) looked with some favour on the idea. It was also true, however, that virtually all prominent politicians and soldiers agreed with Lord Lansdowne, who said in the House of Lords that 'the country was not yet ripe for the change'.[59] Several years later he wrote more candidly to Andrew Bonar Law: 'My own opinion is that some form of compulsory service is inevitable; but such a proposal would, I am afraid, not be popular, and I am not at all sure that as a Party we are prepared to back it up.'[60] In fact he was *quite* sure, and no leader of the Conservative Party ever openly advocated mandatory service in the years before the Great War.

In 1910, as ever, Roberts was optimistic about the National Service campaign, writing to Leo Maxse that 'as soon as the [January] election is over I hope there will be a general movement in the aid of National Defence.'[61] Yet that year was one of tumult greater even than the old soldier could have imagined, and one which saw him temporarily distracted from his compulsory service campaign.

In the first place, King Edward VII died, and the new King, George V, chose Bobs to announce his ascension to the courts of Europe — this took him away from Britain for several months. More revealing was the battle over the reduction of the political powers of the House of Lords. It began with their rejection of the contentious Lloyd George Budget of 1909, and became a full-scale constitutional crisis after the two elections of 1910 in which the political role of the Lords was a major issue.[62] Roberts abhorred the notion of single-chamber rule, which is what the Liberal reform measures destroying the Lords' unconditional veto meant to him. He did not, however, support the continuation of the upper house in the form it then took. He preferred, with Lord Lansdowne, a much smaller body made up of members nominated by the Commons, the full body of peers and the Crown. The Liberals, however, would have none of it, and the Parliament Bill was brought in and passed. Roberts took his stand with Lords Halsbury and Willoughby de Broke and the other 'ditchers' — and went down to defeat. In a letter to *The Times* explaining his decision, he justified the resistance movement in military terms:

> I am prepared to believe that, in politics as in war, the path of duty is also the path of safety. An outpost suddenly attacked

by an overwhelming force may not be able to save itself from capture by resisting. But if it does its duty and resists to the utmost it may give the main body a warning and an opportunity to rally, and the position which the enemy has rushed may soon be re-occupied . . . By doing its duty the House of Lords may not now be able to prevent the Parliament Bill from being carried, but it may awaken the nation to the real nature of the revolution which is in progress, check its further course, and make possible its reversal in the near future.[63]

Bobs' hope was that by taking up the unpopular case in the House of Lords — despite two lost elections — he and his colleagues could give a warning to the nation of what he considered the dangerous innovation of the Parliament Act. In the end he failed, yet, as in the case of his fight for mandatory service, defeat did not deter him in the least.

Roberts was no man of letters, nor had he ever claimed that words were his best weapons. As we have noted, however, from time to time he took to the platform or to print in order to aid his causes. Such a case arose late in the year and brought him back to the conscription campaign. In November 1910, as the crisis over the House of Lords was in full cry, there appeared in the bookstalls a brief work by General Sir Ian Hamilton, with a lengthy foreword by R. B. Haldane, called *Compulsory service: a study of the question in the light of experience.* Hamilton was, along with Sir John French, one of the few soldiers of high rank who actively opposed the notion of peacetime compulsory training. He was also the former aide-de-camp to Roberts from India days and as close to the old soldier as a son.[64]

The book addressed the arguments of the National Service League one by one and set out to demolish them: a conscript force, Hamilton suggested, would be too expensive and too inadequately trained to be much good to an insular island power. While he left the door open to the possibility of wartime compulsion, Sir Ian dismissed as unnecessary the peacetime mandatory service called for time and again by his former mentor.

Roberts was quick to parry Hamilton's thrust: within a matter of months he, Leopold Amery and Professor J. A. Cramb rushed into print *Fallacies and facts: an answer to 'Compulsory Service'*. Charging Hamilton and Haldane with shortsightedness in refusing to see that the time to train armies was *before* any possible conflict, this NSL 'brains trust' also heaped abuse on the War

Secretary for employing the services of a serving officer — two in the second edition, which included an appendix by Admiral Sir Arthur Wilson — to argue political questions in public print.

The glare of celebrity, even when he was merely a non-political soldier-hero, was rather uncomfortable for Bobs; yet in these last years of his long life he uncharacteristically courted controversy and quietly accepted the cheers and reproaches which accompanied the role. He did so for the simplest reasons: his raising of the invasion question before the CID, his leadership of the National Service League, his attempt to co-operate with Haldane and his efforts to pass a non-partisan mandatory service law through Parliament had all failed. More than ever convinced that Britain was unprepared for and vulnerable to the possibility of invasion, and certain that the only potential enemy in a future war of Great Powers was Germany, Lord Roberts, then nearing eighty years of age, began a final propaganda campaign to bring the nation to what he felt were its senses.[65]

Bobs took on the rigours of a speaking tour which did not miss one of the great traditional enclaves of Gladstonianism. As the Balkan Wars tormented south-eastern Europe and yet another crisis brought the Great Powers close to conflict in the Middle East, the elderly field-marshal put the issue of mandatory service into the newspapers as never before. In Manchester, in the autumn of 1912, he spoke about Britain's neighbours and of the possibility of war. As Denis Hayes has written: 'The interest of the great mass of the British public [in conscription], quiet and largely inarticulate, can be dated from October 22nd, 1912, when Lord Roberts addressed a large audience in the Free Trade Hall, Manchester.'[66] In his speech Roberts brought together British anxieties about mandatory service, the possibility of invasion and German 'aggressiveness' and sounded a sombre warning:

> Now, gentlemen, at the present day, now in the year 1912, just as in 1866 and just as in 1870 [the years, respectively, of the German assaults on Austria and France], war will take place the instant German forces by land and sea are, by their superiority at every point, as certain of victory as anything in human calculation can be made certain. 'Germany strikes when Germany's hour has struck.' That is the time-honoured policy of her Foreign Office. That was the policy relentlessly pursued by Bismarck and Moltke in 1866 and 1870; it has been her policy decade by decade since that date; it is her

policy at the present hour . . .

Gentlemen, only the other day I completed my eightieth year . . . and the words I am speaking to-day are, therefore old words — the result of years of earnest thought and practical experience. But Gentlemen, my fellow-citizens and fellow Britishers, citizens of this great and sacred trust, this Empire, if these were my last words, I still say to you — 'arm yourselves' and if I put to myself the question, How can I, even at this late and solemn hour, best help England — England that to me has been so much, England that for me has done so much — again I say, 'Arm yourselves like men for the day of your ordeal is at hand.'[67]

The speech was alternately praised and condemned in the press and Roberts either celebrated or abused, depending upon the editorial policy of the journal. There was, however, agreement among all but the most angry of leader-writers that the octagenarian hero spoke the deepest-held of his convictions — as he did again in Bristol and Wolverhampton and many other cities across the nation before the tour wound up in May 1913.[68]

Despite the growing national concern over the ambitions of Germany, and despite the phenomenal growth of the National Service League, Roberts's campaign was a failure. While his fears of invasion of the home islands in the event of general European war proved groundless, he was absolutely right in warning the nation that a great war would require a trained citizenry and that voluntarism could not produce an army of sufficient size. When the World War came, Roberts was near the end of his long life; he who had lived to see so much would not live to see Britain turn to mandatory military service for the first time in modern history.[35]

There remained in the year of life left to Lord Roberts but one final struggle, and it touched him at least as deeply as his battles for army reform or mandatory military service. This crisis combined the issues of Ulster Unionism, the movement to keep Northern Ireland within the United Kingdom, and the independence of the army itself from what was to him unconstitutional political interference. No concern came closer to his heart. Put most briefly, the Catholic majority of Ireland, led by John Redmond and the Irish National Party, sought political autonomy within the bounds of the Empire. Situated in the north-eastern quarter of the island was the sizeable and politically powerful Protestant minority, whose leaders were Sir Edward Carson and the Ulster Unionist Party, and who opposed Home Rule from Catholic Dublin with a bitter fanaticism which equalled that of the most extreme of Redmond's followers. By early 1914, under the provisions of the Parliament Act of 1911, which diluted the Lords' veto over legislation, Irish Home Rule was close to becoming law.

Roberts was by blood an Anglo-Irishman and, while he had lived there only briefly, he staunchly considered Dublin as much a part of Great Britain as London, Edinburgh or Cardiff. Like so many of his breed who had risen through the ranks of the service, he was a loyal Protestant, passionate about the Empire he had served for more than half a century. His feelings already inflamed by following the seemingly inevitable progress of the Home Rule Bill toward the law-books, he was even more troubled by the rumours among Unionists that the Liberal Government intended to employ troops to force Home Rule upon an unwilling Ulster. It appeared that Ulster meant to resist; for as early as September 1912, in a great meeting in their stronghold of Belfast and with much show of support from British sympathisers, there was adopted an Ulster Covenant — symbolic of willingness to follow a provisional Protestant government rather than a Dublin Parliament in case of the passage of Home Rule.[69] Futhermore (as Catholics did the same in the south) a private army calling itself the Ulster Volunteer Force was formed and began drilling in village commons. Fearing a 'pogrom' of the Ulstermen by the Liberal Government he so distrusted, Roberts lent his imprimatur to the movement by supplying the Volunteer Force with a proper commander, one General Sir George Richardson, whom he persuaded to accept the post. In April 1914, when there were no legal bars left to the passage of the Home Rule Bill, Roberts accepted the presidency of the loose organisation of British supporters of the Ulster Covenant. He was not alone among notables taking so intransigent a position, for joining him were Lord Milner, Lord Halifax, F. E. Smith, the poet Kipling, the composer Sir Edward Elgar and many thousands of others.[70]

Certainly the most infamous moment in this affair was what has come to be called the 'Curragh Mutiny', in which a substantial number of officers of the British Army in Ireland, based at the Curragh near Dublin, indicated their preference for resignation or even dismissal to the possibility of taking any action to force Home Rule on Ulster.[71] The confusion of this affair, due in part to the bungling of Haldane's successor at the War Office, J. E. B. Seeley, and to the inappropriate demands of the clearly pro-Ulster officer corps of the army in Ireland, resulted in the weakening of the Government's hand over Irish policy. Heightening tensions even more was the fact that both of the unauthorised para-military forces in Ireland were attempting to import illegal firearms in preparation for armed struggle over Home Rule. If armed civil disturbances did follow on the heels of the bill, as appeared likely, then the army would be needed to restore order. An army with no officer corps was, of course, no army at all — and was no use to the Government.

For Roberts, no political or military crisis in his long life caused him more anxiety than did this episode. The Catholic Irish, he agreed, had suffered many wrongs which required redress. To break up the United Kingdom, however, was to him a step so wrong-headed that it violated the historical integrity of the nation itself. He blamed the Liberal Government which had, in his eyes, sold the national birthright to maintain its political success.

Accused unjustly by Seeley of instigating the Curragh affair, Bobs made no secret of the fact that he thought the attempt to force Home Rule on Ulster could virtually destroy the Army. On the other hand, the idea that the Army should be, from his viewpoint, dragged openly into partisan politics was devastating to him.[72] To him, soldiers pledged to protect the dominions of the Crown were being forced to choose between the legal authority of their political masters on the one hand, and their sense of duty on the other. He told the House of Lords in his last speech:

> Discipline may be of such well-conceived strength as is indeed the case of our Army, that it will dominate and override human nature under almost every imaginable circumstance; it has inherent in itself the weakness of its artificiality, and it labours under this initial disadvantage when pitted against natural instincts. So much so is this the case that if you penetrate deep enough into the depths of human nature you will unfailingly reach in each one of us a stratum which is impervious to discipline or any other influence from without. The strongest manifestation of this truth lies in what men call conscience — an innate sense of right and wrong, which neither reason nor man-made laws can affect.
>
> I know full well that some people scoff at the idea that the Army can be actuated by motives of conscience; others claim that soldiers should be devoid of conscience. In reasoning thus, they divorce themselves from realities, for they forget that soldiers are but human beings.[73]

Put most simply, for him the national crisis was a matter of conscience in which the army he loved was in danger of being pulled apart by the alternate forces of duty and conscience. Within a matter of weeks, however, even these grave circumstances paled next to the greater crisis of the World War. Appointed honorary Colonel-in-Chief of Overseas Forces, Bobs died in November 1914, as he would have wished, close to the battle line in France and visiting the Indian regiments by which he is to this day remembered. Perhaps the greatest irony of all was that little more than a year later, Britain implemented her first mandatory military service law of modern times — in a way, the old soldier was right all along.

Frederick Sleigh Roberts brought to the twentieth century all of the moral and intellectual baggage of the Victorian age in which he was born and in which he prospered. He sought, by his own lights, to protect and conserve the vital elements of the world that he knew best — the Empire and the Army. He feared no man and no idea and never shrank from a fight with either. In his last years he risked his enviable reputation and dared to strike off in politically unacceptable — certainly untraditional — directions. He did so not as a conservative-turned-reactionary who sought to renew the past, but as a true conservative who wished to adapt the best elements of the past to the present. He failed not for want of trying but because, in the first place, the modern world did not place a similar value on his Empire and its guardians. Secondly, he neither understood nor mastered the ways of political democracy. To his credit, unlike some conservatives in his and other times, he did not attempt to subvert it. As could be said of others among the subjects of these essays, it was a kindness that his long, full life ended when it did.

Notes

1. David James, *Lord Roberts* (Hollis and Carter, London, 1959), p. 8.
2. For the development and organisation of the Indian Army, see Phillip Mason, *A matter of honour* (Jonathan Cape, London, 1974), and Roger Beaumont, *Sword of the Raj* (Bobbs-Merrill, New York, 1977).
3. William Manchester, *The last lion: Winston Spencer Churchill, Vol. I: Visions of glory, 1874–1932* (Dell, New York, 1983), p. 222.
4. James, *Lord Roberts*, p. 23.
5. After the Mutiny, the Crown took on the political powers of the East India Company. The office of Governor-General was abolished and

a Viceroy, who received his Government's instructions through Her Majesty's Secretary of State for India, became the chief executive of Indian government.

6. Brigadier The Rt Hon. Sir John Smyth, Bt, *The story of the Victoria Cross, 1856–1963* (Frederick Muller, London, 1966), pp. 70–1.

7. The brevet rank system allowed officers to assume the responsibilities in their units of ranks higher than their own without the parsimonious government having to pay them the higher salaries which accompanied permanent promotion. Consequently, lieutenants did the work of majors, majors acted as brigadier-generals and colonels did the duties of major-generals.

8. The most recent study of the Magdala campaign is Darrell Bates, *The Abyssinian difficulty* (Oxford University Press, Oxford, 1979).

9. James, *Lord Roberts*, pp. 108–9.

10. Ibid., p. 127.

11. National Army Museum, London. Roberts Papers. Portions of this letter are printed in ibid., p. 151.

12. Roberts Papers.

13. James, *Lord Roberts*, p. 162.

14. Ibid., p. 163.

15. Because of his views on Army reform, Wolseley's name was usually linked with the Liberals and he certainly benefited from the association, but privately he detested Gladstone and the Radicals 'because they are churchwardens and parish vestrymen more than Englishmen'. He kept his feelings to himself, however. See Joseph H. Lehmann, *All Sir Garnet: a life of Field-Marshal Lord Wolseley* (Jonathan Cape, London, 1964), pp. 282–3.

16. For the Cardwell army reforms, see Edward M. Spiers, *The Army and society, 1815–1914* (Longman, London, 1980), pp. 170–205.

17. In March 1881, following the disastrous defeat of Sir George Colley at Majuba Hill, Roberts was sent to South Africa as Governor of Natal and Commander-in-Chief, British Forces. Before he arrived, however, peace was negotiated, and he returned immediately to London, and soon thereafter to India.

18. Like Kitchener fifteen years later, Roberts dreamed of succeeding to the viceroyalty when it became open in 1884, but there is no evidence to suggest that the appointment was ever contemplated.

19. This was published in 1895 as *The rise of Wellington* and enjoyed a brisk sale.

20. For Wolseley's succession to the Duke, see Lehmann, *All Sir Garnet*, pp. 382–5; and Jay Luvaas, *The education of an army: British military thought, 1815–1940* (University of Chicago Press, Chicago, 1964), pp. 271–2, n. 32.

21. Thomas Packenham, *The Boer War* (Weidenfeld and Nicolson, London, 1979), pp. 253–4.

22. Roberts, unknowingly, had the opportunity to capture the presidents of both Boer republics, Paul Krueger and Marthinus Stein. Only the tardiness of his cavalry contingent — commanded, ironically, by the ill-starred John French — prevented the coup. See Richard Holmes, *The little Field-Marshal: Sir John French* (Jonathan Cape, London, 1981), pp. 97–101.

23. The Orange Free State was officially annexed on 24 October 1900, the Queen's birthday.

24. Lord Wolseley had begun to show the symptoms of what was probably Alzheimer's disease. See Lehmann, *All Sir Garnet*, pp. 385–8.

25. Spiers, *Army and society*, p. 246.

26. Ibid., pp. 247–8.

27. Roberts Papers, 12 February 1904. Portions printed in James, *Lord Roberts*, p. 402.

28. The best illustrative source on the spirit of the time remains George Dangerfield, *The strange death of Liberal England*, 2nd edn (Capricorn Books, New York, 1961). Also excellent is Samuel Hynes, *The Edwardian turn of mind* (Princeton University Press, Princeton, New Jersey, 1968).

29. *Parliamentary Debates*, 4th Series, House of Lords, vol. CXCVI, col. 1695. See James, *Lord Roberts*, p. 435.

30. A fuller discussion of this issue may be found in R. J. Q. Adams, 'The National Service League and mandatory service in Edwardian Britain', *Armed Forces and Society* [U.S.A.], vol. 12, no. 1, Fall 1985.

31. Le Queux wrote the book to order for the press lord, Lord Northcliffe, and it was serialised in his newspapers.

32. Le Queux wrote to Lord Roberts in 1906 complaining at the violent opposition his book generated. Roberts replied that people also thought he was a lunatic! See A. J. A. Morris, *The scaremongers: the advocacy of war and rearmament, 1896–1914* (Routledge and Kegan Paul, London, 1984), p. 157.

33. *The invasion of 1910* was not Le Queux's first 'scaremongering' novel. For his career and the genre of such fiction see I. F. Clarke, *Voices prophesying war* (Oxford University Press, Oxford, 1966).

34. Zara Steiner, *Britain and the origins of the First World War* (London, St Martin's Press, 1977), p. 156.

35. Morris, *Scaremongers*, p. 377.

36. For the significance of the youth movements see John Springhall, *Youth, empire and society: British youth movements, 1883–1940* (Croom Helm, London, 1977), and Ann Summers, 'Militarism in Britain before the Great War', *History Workshop Journal*, no. 3 (August 1976).

37. When recruitment figures fell below estimates, which they often did, the most common short-term remedy was to lower physical requirements for enlistment. In 1900, standards required that recruits be at least eighteen years of age, 115 pounds in weight and five feet three inches in height. Despite these modest criteria, almost one-third of those enlisted from 1890 to 1900 failed to meet them and were recruited on special dispensations issued by Army physicians. See Alan Ramsay Skelley, *The Victorian army at home: the recruitment and terms and conditions of the British regular, 1859–1899* (Croom Helm, London, 1977), p. 238. Roberts was already campaigning to improve recruiting standards and practices as early as 1884. Spiers, *Army and society*, p. 27.

38. Balfour revealed this information to the House of Commons on 16 May 1901. *Parliamentary debates*, 4th Series, House of Commons, vol. XC, cols. 382–3.

39. See John Gooch, *Plans of war: the General Staff and British military strategy c. 1900–1916* (Routledge and Kegan Paul, London, 1974), pp. 278–9.

40. *Draft report on the possibility of serious invasion: home defence*, 11 November 1903. CAB 3/1/18A.

41. See Lord Roberts, 'The Army — as it was and as it is', *The Nineteenth Century — and After*, LVII, January 1905.

42. For the conscription issue in this period see Denis Hayes, *Conscription conflict* (Sheppard Press, London, 1949). More recently, Morris, *The Scaremongers*, has dealt with the question up to 1914, and R. J. Q. Adams and Philip P. Poirier, *The conscription controversy in Great Britain, 1900–18* (Macmillan, London, 1987) have treated it through the World War.

43. Roberts presented a paper on 3 November 1905 calling for mandatory cadet training for schoolboys and rifle drill for youths, CAB 38/78. Delighted to be done with him, Balfour disingenuously wrote to Bobs pleading with him to withdraw his resignation, though he had earlier lamented to H. O. Arnold-Forster: 'Of course, we cannot get rid of the old man.' Peter Fraser, *Lord Esher* (Rupert Hart-Davis, London, 1973), p. 159.

44. For these figures see *The Times*, 29 June 1910, and *The Spectator*, 7 August 1914. See also Adams, 'National Service League and mandatory service'.

45. Roberts, *The Nineteenth Century*.

46. F. S. Oliver, *Ordeal by battle*, abridged edition (Macmillan, London, 1916), p. X.

47. Fraser, *Lord Esher*, p. 159.

48. See *The Times*, 27 June 1911.

49. Lord Roberts to Leopold Maxse, 19 June 1912, West Sussex Record Office, Chichester, Maxse Papers 466.

50. Lord Roberts to Andrew Bonar Law, 16 March 1903, House of Lords Record Office, London, Bonar Law Papers, 29/2/25. Among the front-bench Liberals, only Lloyd George and Churchill were willing to entertain seriously the idea of mandatory service, though even these 'terrible twins' kept silent on the issue. Conscription rather like Roberts's plan was included in the famous Lloyd George memorandum of 1910, though this, of course, was not made known to the full parliamentary party, much less to the public. The memorandum is printed as an appendix in John Grigg, *Lloyd George: the people's champion, 1902–1911* (Methuen, London, 1978). J. E. B. Seeley, who succeeded Haldane at the War Office, had been a founding member of the National Service League but appears to have given up the idea when he left the Tory Party to join the Liberals over the tariff-reform campaign.

51. While frustrated from the outset by the limitations of the Haldane scheme, Roberts referred to the programme as 'the greatest step forward in the direction of a national army which has ever been made officially'. *The Times*, 3 April 1907. For the entirety of the Haldane reforms, see Edward Spiers, *Haldane: an Army reformer* (Edinburgh University Press, Edinburgh, 1980).

52. The amending bill was soundly defeated on its first reading, regarding which the League's house organ observed that history taught that such frequently was the case 'in regard to the first Bill in which any reform has been embodied'. *The Nation in Arms*, August 1908. See also Hayes, *Conscription conflict*, pp. 88–9. For the place of Kincaid-Smith in

the conscription campaign, see Morris, *Scaremongers*, pp. 235–8.

53. In this regard, see G. R. Searle, *The quest for national efficiency* (Blackwell, Oxford, 1971).

54. See W. Michael Ryan, 'The invasion controversy of 1906–1908', *Military Affairs* [USA], February 1980.

55. The report of the committee was published in 1908, CAB 16/3A.

56. Michael Howard, *The Continental commitment: the dilemma of British defence policy in the era of the two world wars* (Penguin, Harmondsworth, 1971), p. 38. For the invasion and spy panic, see Morris, *Scaremongers*, p. 161.

57. Balfour, who remained opposed to conscription, quite willingly conspired with Haldane to make certain that the Tories did not take up Roberts's bill. Spiers, *An Army Reformer*, p. 171.

58. General Ian Hamilton wrote to Lady Roberts in December 1910 that the entire Imperial General Staff favoured conscription on the 'Continental basis'. See Adams and Poirier, *Conscription controversy*, p. 27.

59. James, *Lord Roberts*, p. 439.

60. 6 July 1912, Bonar Law Papers, 26 May 1911.

61. 1 January 1910, Maxse Papers, 461.

62. For the struggle over the House of Lords, see Roy Jenkins, *Mr Balfour's poodle* (Heinemann, London, 1954), and Dangerfield, *Strange death*.

63. *The Times*, 8 August 1911.

64. Hamilton was, at the time the book was written, Inspector General of Overseas Forces; and no one hated him more for his 'treachery' to his old commander and to the Army than Bobs's unqualified admirer, Rudyard Kipling, who wrote to his cousin, the future premier Stanley Baldwin:

> When Haldane's Hound upon Haldane's hobbies
> Writes a book which is full of lies
> Then we find out what a first class job is
> And how Inspector Generals rise.

Morris, *Scaremongers*, p. 243.

65. Lord Roberts to R. D. Blumenfeld, 22 September 1912, House of Lords Record Office, London, Blumenfeld Papers.

66. Hayes, *Conscription conflict*, p. 111.

67. *The Times*, 23 October 1912.

68. In the spring of 1913 Roberts was again optimistic that the tide of public and political opinion was turning toward compulsion. See Morris, *Scaremongers*, pp. 332–3.

69. George Dangerfield, *The damnable question: a study in Anglo-Irish relations* (Little Brown, New York, 1976), p. 76.

70. A. M. Gollin, *Proconsul in politics: a study of Lord Milner in opposition and in power* (Anthony Blond, London, 1964), p. 212.

71. The theme that the Army was in danger of being torn apart by politicians (as opposed to politics) in a time of national danger was the central argument in Lord Roberts's privately printed pamphlet, *Ulster and the Army*. A copy is preserved in the Roberts Papers.

72. *Parliamentary debates*, 5th Series, House of Lords, vol. XVI, cols. 715–19.

4
Lord Willoughby de Broke: Radicalism and Conservatism*

Gregory D. Phillips

In the midst of the political controversies of the early twentieth century, Lord Willoughby de Broke, a landed aristocrat with little parliamentary experience, emerged as a major political figure. An ally of the Chamberlains, Lord Milner, Sir Edward Carson, and Leo Maxse, editor of the *Nation Review*, he became a significant spokesman for extreme conservatism. During the Parliament Bill struggle, the battle over the Conservative leadership in the fall of 1911, and the Home Rule crisis, Willoughby de Broke organised the efforts of peers and other Conservatives who were radically dissatisfied with the direction of British politics.

Since 1914 Willoughby de Broke has become a symbol of traditionalist resistance to change: the fox-hunting nobleman 'whose face', in Dangerfield's well-known description, 'bore a pleasing resemblance to the horse', and who 'was not more than two hundred years behind his time'.[1] Such an analysis, however, is more amusing than accurate. It focuses entirely on Willoughby de Broke's expressed fondness for the patriarchal society he had known in his childhood on a great landed estate and on his passion for the pursuit of the fox. It ignores his recognition of the troubled political conditions of the early twentieth century and his belief that Conservatives must master the tactics of political democracy in order to triumph over the enemies of a well-ordered society at home and of British power in the world at large. Willoughby de Broke constantly justified his political tactics during the period 1909 to 1914 by referring to their appeal for the electorate as a whole. He was convinced that the vast majority of ordinary people were conservatives at heart and strayed from their natural political home in the Conservative Party only when the party leadership failed to provide clear guidance.[2] Indeed, Willoughby de Broke and his associates justified their resort to extreme methods, including the encouragement of violent resistance to the Liberal government, on the grounds that, in the era of mass politics, only such extreme tactics provided politicians with the notoriety which was all-important to electoral success. Arthur Balfour and the Marquess of Lansdowne, the official Conservative leadership, were dismissed as ineffectual compromisers, lukewarm to tariff reform, conscription, national defence, Ireland, and the powers of the House of Lords. These leaders had to be replaced by others willing to adopt unyielding attitudes which would attract a larger, more committed following.

Willoughby de Broke's family background was typical of his class. His family owned over 18,000 acres, mostly in southern Warwickshire. His predecessors were staunch, almost instinctive Tories interested in their estate and in foxhunting. It was into an intensely traditional milieu that Richard Grenville Verney, the future nineteenth Baron Willoughby de Broke, was born in 1869, and throughout his political career he looked with nostalgic longing to the patriarchal society he had known in his childhood, in which he had come to appreciate what he saw as 'that real treasure, the bond of love between master and man'.[3]

Almost from the first, however, discordant elements intruded on Willoughby de Broke's world. He noted later that his home was 'too close to Birmingham to be pleasant for a peer'.[4] The geographical juxtaposition of radical Birmingham with Willoughby's family seat symbolised a host of factors threatening landed society. Agricultural depression hit England in the 1870s and the estate gradually became 'over burdened' with charges and mortgages.[5] During the same period local-government reforms established elected councils, which required more effort from the aristocrats to maintain their former position, and 'Parliamentary elections', Willoughby de Broke perceived, 'ceased to be a choice between a Whig and a Tory landlord; the squire was opposed by the Radical . . . out to demolish the existing order'.[6]

Willoughby de Broke's education at Eton and Oxford did nothing to broaden his political horizons or his social circles. Of his university, where he spent much of his time foxhunting, he later wrote that 'the schemer, the prig and the bore will find more others like unto themselves at Oxford than they will find anywhere else all through their lives'.[7] His school years did leave him with the uneasy feeling that the pre-eminent position of England was being seriously challenged by other powers. In few places was this national threat more emphasised than at the Eton of his day, under the headmastership of the militantly patriotic Edmund Warre, and this heightened sense of England's insecurity had important psychological effects for Willoughby de Broke. He sensed that at the same time both the landed society of his youth and the entire British empire were under attack.[8] This perception of simultaneous crises which called for immediate action contributed to a tendency to divide the political world into opposing camps of friends and enemies. This crisis situation and a highly developed sense of duty inculcated from childhood impelled him to take an activist political role. He was convinced that lofty status entailed great responsibilities; that in the distant past, 'Rank was conferred on a man and his heirs for service to the state,' and that he could justify his position only if he provided leadership for his society.[9]

Willoughby de Broke began his rise to prominence in an atmosphere of muted dissension among Conservatives after the Liberal election triumph of 1906.[10] He associated himself closely with the *National Review*, which became the centre for attacks on the leadership, and he soon took an important place in a growing network of Conservative activists. Disagreement about the wisdom of adopting a protectionist programme damaged relations between Balfour and the more extreme members of his party. Willoughby de Broke and other Conservatives fervently opposed the innovative taxes contained in the Lloyd George budget of 1909 and regarded protection as a vastly preferable means of raising revenue for armaments and social programmes.[11] Many landed aristocrats who might otherwise have been expected to have little use for the Chamberlains supported them wholeheartedly because of a belief that a tariff-reform policy would ensure Unionist electoral victories. From early 1909 through the two election campaigns of 1910, Willoughby de Broke preached tariff reform from platforms throughout the country. He did so because he believed that tariff reform was all the working class 'really cared about'.[12] In 1910 he told Leo Maxse that Unionists would surely defeat the Liberals if they played 'the ace of Tariff Reform and Colonial Preference'.[13]

Having been repeatedly frustrated with their leaders over tariff reform and other issues, some Conservatives suspected that Balfour and Lansdowne might compromise with the Liberal government during the House of Lords crisis in 1910.[14] Any compromise on the issue of the Lords, Willoughby de Broke and his colleagues believed, would demoralise the Conservative electorate.

Willoughby de Broke had warned Maxse earlier that 'our only hope is to fight like blazes against enemies within and without'.[15] During the late summer and early autumn of 1910, evidence of discontent surfaced in Leo Maxse's articles in the *National Review*. In July, Willoughby de Broke had told Maxse that he looked foreward to attacking the Liberals in the autumn but had heard of 'a party that called themselves Unionists who want to stay their hand from motives of expediency'. He warned that the 'people are sick of tactics'.[16] In August, he urged Maxse to 'kill' the notion that 'the Rads are to be nursed in Parliament till it suits certain people to throw them out . . . If our present leaders do not take care, a middle party of Tories who mean business will smash them.'[17] Maxse adopted this line in his column, noting that there was 'too much tactics and too little strategy'.[18] More experienced politicians privately agreed that Unionists needed to allay fears about their 'solidity or . . . consistency'. The Earl of Selborne, formerly First Lord of the Admiralty and Milner's successor as high commissioner in South Africa, told Balfour: 'We have a splendid programme: The essential thing is not to vary it . . . The reputation to aim at . . . is that of a "rock of principle".'[19] By late August 1910, even Lord Curzon, later vilified by the Diehards for his position on the Parliament Bill, deplored Balfour's 'extraordinary reluctance . . . to fulfil the ordinary functions of a leader'.[20]

From October 1910, public criticism of Balfour and the official leadership became more pointed, yet stopped short of demands for resignation. Maxse demanded that the 'Old Gang' take more interest in the party. He urged Balfour to direct his comments to the majority of the public 'educated in our elementary schools', rather than to the few 'educated at the Universities'.[21] Dissatisfaction in parliamentary circles with Balfour and Lansdowne took formal shape in October 1910 when Willoughby de Broke, together with Henry Page Croft, soldier and Unionist MP, and other tariff reformers, organised a 'Reveille' group to 'rouse the Unionist party without forsaking Unionist principles'. A manifesto praised and published by the *National Review* demanded tariff reform, the formulation of other Conservative policies, and emphasised the 'democratic' nature of the party.[22] Most observers believed that the programme of this group constituted an attack on the Unionist leadership. After some explanation, however, the 'Reveille' group's plans to foster electoral enthusiasm were approved by Lansdowne and the party agents, although the former told Willoughby de Broke, perhaps ironically, that it was 'a little unfortunate that your object should . . . have been misapprehended'.[23]

Until late July 1911, Willoughby de Broke continued to hope that the leadership would fight the Parliament Bill, and he worked to stiffen its resolve against compromise.[24] Although he stated in his autobiography that 'the actual "ditcher" movement was only conceived within three weeks of the final struggle in the Lords', preliminary organisational activities began in mid-June.[25] Early in that month George Wyndham, the former chief secretary for Ireland and one of the firmest opponents of accommodation with Liberalism, had written to Willoughby de Broke that the Conservative peers could save the situation if they would meet and resolve to 'fight for giving the people . . . a chance of a see & a say on great changes, before those changes were imposed by the Cabinet & the Caucus'. If the peers did this, then 'Commoners would rally great forces in the country'.[26] Wyndham urged Willoughby de Broke 'to "recruit" those Peers' who would 'fight to the end, even if the leadership counsel surrender'.[27]

The extensive canvassing of peers that began in mid-June had two objects: to obtain signatures to a resolution urging Lansdowne to be firm in his opposition to the Liberals, and to organise defiance in the event that the party leadership compromised. Numerous reports of potential support reached Willoughby de Broke from peers around the country.[28] By 19 June he could report to Maxse that they had 'a body of 35 to 40 already' who supported their efforts.[29] Willoughby de Broke made his appeal to a broad political cross-section of the peerage, including those who opposed all change and those who were more flexible in their attitudes toward reform. He told Maxse that he had decided to urge a purposely ambiguous amendment to the Parliament Bill, that 'after a third rejection by the House of Lords a Bill shall not become law until it has been submitted and approved by the Electors'. A subsection to the amendment would define this process as either a general election or a referendum. Although Willoughby de Broke was personally opposed to the idea of a referendum, he was aware that it was popular in some circles, especially with the influential Lord Selborne. By proposing his ambiguous amendment, Willoughby de Broke hoped to attract the support of the 'Referendumites' and 'not tie our hands to the infernal thing altogether'.[30]

Willoughby de Broke, working with Selborne and Maxse, under the nominal leadership of the Earl of Halsbury, made himself the principal organiser and strategist of the 'ditchers', the peers who voted against the Parliament Bill. To Willoughby de Broke, this measure represented the culmination of a Liberal 'war upon the Constitution of this country' that would enable the government to capitalise on the politics of class and facilitate the passage of Home Rule.[31] He repeatedly accused the Liberal government of acting from the basest party motives. The peers were trustees for the nation in 'a struggle between the Cabinet and the vast body of opinion which still realises what free government means in a free country'.[32]

At a meeting of the shadow cabinet on 21 July, the Conservative leadership decided to abandon its opposition to the Parliament Bill in the face of the Liberal government's revelation that it had the King's promise to create enough peers to swamp the upper chamber. At a meeting of peers the same day, Lord Halsbury denounced the policy of surrender and was supported by Willoughby de Broke and Lord Milner, among others. Milner had not previously taken an active role, but had informed Selborne before the 21st that he would join 'any group of peers who really mean to fight to the end'.[33] The 'ditchers' thus gained an important ally, and Willoughby de Broke established close contact with a leading political figure who fully shared his distaste for compromise. After the shadow cabinet meeting, the work of canvassing and rallying support gained a new urgency.[34] On the 21st, Willoughby de Broke told Maxse in confidence that the Duke of Westminster had given their forces a room in Grosvenor House 'to whip from'.[35]

The 'ditchers' decision to defy their Party's leadership and vote against the Parliament Bill was based on much more than a fervent desire to maintain the prerogatives of the Lords: the more politically sophisticated among their number also justified their course of action on the grounds of political tactics. Uppermost in their minds was the effect of determined resistance on the voters and the country at large.[36] Throughout the struggle, the ditchers' goal was to boost the morale of the Conservative Party and thereby pave the way to future electoral victories. After smashing the Liberal government, Unionists could repeal the Parliament Act even if it passed over their opposition.

The ditchers sensed that the electorate had responded apathetically to the two elections of 1910. Willoughby de Broke argued that a dramatic stand against the Parliament Bill would alert the country to the great changes taking place. Publicity would lead to outrage, and an aroused public opinion would prevent further sweeping alterations in government. The Parliament Bill crisis was merely one phase in a 'prolonged Constitutional conflict' that would continue 'for a great many years to come'.[37] Selborne similarly emphasised the need for publicity, stating that 'the greatest evil which can befall a nation is to have its constitutional stability destroyed by a revolution and not to know it'.[38] Lord Ampthill urged that Unionist peers must start 'to explain' to the country 'how the People have actually been robbed of their liberties'.[39]

If the Parliament Bill issue was part of a long-term battle to save the country from Radicalism or worse, then it was necessary to do everything to strengthen the will and increase the numbers of the Conservative Party. The ditchers believed that a strong stand would inspire the rank-and-file. If peers did not act to preserve their integrity, their appeals to the electorate would inevitably fail. The Earl of Clarendon told Willoughby de Broke: 'to give way . . . will be absolutely fatal to the interests of the Unionist Party in the country'. Unless the peers made 'a struggle for existence' the electorate would abandon the Conservative cause.[40] The Duke of Somerset had declared earlier that compromise would mean that the 'Country now has a perfect right to say — you are a useless lot of cowards — for God's sake shut up your house & go.'[41]

Implicit in much correspondence and rhetoric in the days before the division on the bill of 10 August was the assumption that attracting publicity by taking a strong stand was at least as important as defeating the Liberal forces on this particular issue. The Diehards recognised that the peers alone could not successfully resist a powerful Liberal government. They hoped to use the Parliament Bill crisis to awaken and rally the forces of Conservatism. The Liberals' victory on the bill, if it came, would be pyrrhic, as reaction to their policies, highlighted and publicised by ditchers' intransigence, would sweep them out of power. At that point, Unionists, reinvigorated by battle, would correct the balance of the consitution. Willoughby de Broke believed 'the present powers of the House of Lords will be far more difficult to recover if they are surrendered, than if they are taken away by main force'.[42]

The ditchers realised that they could lose the immediate Parliament Bill struggle in one of two ways. Either they could be in the majority in the division, in which case the king might create enough peers — 500 was the figure mentioned — to give the

Liberals an overall majority in the Lords, or else Conservative peers, afraid of the dilution of their order such a creation would bring, might vote with the government in sufficient numbers to pass the bill and avoid the necessity of such a creation. Whichever scenario came to pass, the Diehards believed they would be victorious in the long run. If the ditchers managed to gain the majority in the division, the Liberals might force the king to create 500 peers. These peers could be dealt with in several ways. The elderly Lord Stanmore, long-time colonial administrator, had concluded by late July, after 'years of reading', that the House of Lords could in the future expel the new creations.[43] As with other Unionist opponents of the Parliament Bill, Stanmore believed that in securing the King's pledge to create peers the Liberal cabinet had committed an unconstitutional act. When Unionists returned to power, they could use the illegal quality of the new creations to justify a purge of the upper house. In addition, the controversial 'preamble' to the Parliament Bill, which announced in vague terms an intention to reform the House of Lords, seemed to invite further upheaval. Unionists denounced the preamble as a hypocritical statement inserted by a Radical cabinet to enlist moderate Liberal support. They recognised, however, that the ambiguity of the preamble could work to the advantage of the Conservative Party, allowing for a sweeping change in the membership of the House of Lords and for an eventual restoration of its powers.[44] Alternatively, a peer created as a Radical might not remain so for long. A new peerage had a well-known calming effect. Leo Maxse suggested that within two weeks of the mass creation, large numbers of new peers would begin 'reconsidering' their opinions about the upper chamber. He predicted enough absenteeism among these rapid converts to Conservatism that the Parliament Bill would in any case go down in defeat.[45] The ultimate solution upon which the ditchers depended would be a by-product of their stand on the bill: public outrage, followed by Conservative election triumphs, culminating in the repeal of the Parliament Bill and suitable reform of the House of Lords.

From the day the Conservatives' official leadership decided on abstention on the Parliament Bill division, however, Willoughby de Broke and Maxse suspected that in order to prevent the creation of 500 Liberal peers, the Unionist leaders would enlist Conservative peers to vote for the bill. If the official leaders and their followers, dubbed 'the Court Party' by Willoughby de Broke, and the 'Mandarins' by Maxse, voted with the Liberals, the crisis would serve a double political purpose. In the ditchers, the Conservative Party would have a symbol of principled action to rally around and the party would have the opportunity to purge its weaker, less committed members. As Maxse noted the day after the decision to abstain had been made, 'Mr. Balfour will produce a split if he listens to craven counsellors — that is perhaps a solution[:] Mandarins to the Left, Men to the Right.'[46] Willoughby de Broke had written to Maxse the day before that he believed the 'Court Party' would 'vote for the Bill' rather than suffer the indignity of mass creation: 'This will be right. It will serve the double purpose of stopping the Peers and finally stewing the white-flaggers. They can then go over bodily to the Radicals.'[47] If the Parliament Bill passed with the help of Conservative votes, there would be no mass creation because the Liberals would have achieved their object of destroying the Lords' veto without it; a purified Unionist Party would emerge; and there would be a more even distribution of peers by party, thus removing a major Liberal battle-cry against the House of Lords.

Willoughby de Broke's predictions that some Conservative peers would side with their Liberal colleagues in the Parliament Bill division and that the division would not put an end to the political crisis proved correct. In spite of the ditchers' defeat, Willoughby de Broke's leadership role enhanced his reputation and influence in the party. He received much praise following the stand against the Parliament Bill, and the party leadership considered harnessing his considerable energies for their own purposes.[48] Curzon, Lord Newton, and Arthur Steel-Maitland, principal Conservative party agent, all recommended him at various times to Lansdowne as a possible whip, and Newton later asserted that Willoughby de Broke's importance in dissident movements was so great that 'the split in the party might have been minimized' if he had been brought into the leadership councils.[49] In 1911, perhaps hoping to turn a troublemaker into a member of the establishment, Balfour appointed him to a committee to inquire into the vexed question of Conservative party organisation.[50]

Balfour's choice of Willoughby de Broke for this committee was singularly appropriate, for Willoughby de Broke had been preoccupied with the seeming inability of the Conservative Party to fight elections successfully. Dissatisfaction with the leadership centred by 1911 on the growing belief that the Conservatives could not regain power with Balfour at their head. This belief had been circulating widely for some time in Conservative circles. Complaints focusing on Balfour's lack of enthusiasm for protection and his pledge to submit tariff reform to a referendum before authorising legislation had appeared in print in the *Morning Post* and the *National Review*. In January 1911, Maxse escalated the quarrel by declaring that it would be better for the Unionist party if Balfour resigned. Maxse repeated this opinion in increasingly strident tones, culminating in October 1911 with 'The Champion Scuttler', denouncing the leadership's policy during the Parliament Bill crisis. Maxse argued that the party required someone who would provide a clear, uncomplicated lead in terms the common man would understand, and be willing to take the fight with Liberalism to the country. He held that Balfour was 'as completely out of touch with the "man in the street" as the "man in the street" is out of touch with him . . . Under Mr. Balfour there is little or no hope of the Unionist party regaining its influence in the State.'[51] The leadership was 'tired', having spent too long 'in the enervating and demoralising atmosphere of the House of Commons'. Fatigue meant that Balfour and the other 'Mandarins' of the party would seek compromise to avoid a strenuous fight rather than stand up for the principles of conservatism.[52]

After 10 August the charges against Balfour were elevated from enervation to treason. The leadership was responsible for the 'Judas Iscariot Party' of Unionist peers who voted for the Parliament Bill.[53] Balfour, the 'Champion Scuttler', had weakened the party in the eyes of the average voter by opting for 'tactics' rather than principle

> [The] working man has a healthy contempt for moral cowards . . . The electors of this country are plain people who will never understand the motives of a party which one day votes against the Parliament Bill, the next day votes for it or abstains, and then, when it has passed, proclaims the intention of reversing it. If the Parliament Bill is to be undone . . . if . . . the Unionist Party is ever to return to power, it must find some other leader than Mr. Balfour.[54]

With this article the 'Balfour Must Go' campaign officially began. Balfour had to go because he allegedly failed to realise that the new mass electorate understood only simple ideas and vivid slogans constantly repeated. As Willoughby de Broke had written to Maxse in January, 'The British Constitution . . . is the only thing the Conservative Electors understood . . . First principles, and again First principles are what we must preach . . . No more tactics.'[55]

While the campaign in the pages of the *National Review* mounted in intensity during and after August, a parallel movement had begun within the parliamentary party. In August, Willoughby de Broke began a drive, closely co-ordinated with Maxse, to develop opposition in the peerage to the continued leadership of Balfour and Lansdowne. Like Maxse, but unlike many of his fellow Diehards, Willoughby de Broke had decided by August that a drastic change in the leadership was necessary. Convinced that the ditchers' stand had communicated a new fighting spirit to Conservatives in the country, Willoughby de Broke feared that if Diehards did not refuse to follow their old leaders, then 'the whole fruit of our action will be lost' and 'the suspicion is bound to arise . . . that the whole thing is nothing but a "put up job" '. He believed that the ditchers had succeeded in one of their major objects in opposing the Parliament Bill: they had attracted attention and awakened the electorate to the need for strong, principled action. Denying he had ever been a 'rabid Anti-Balfourite', he told Lord Selborne that he was motivated in his opposition to Balfour by the 'very strong feeling' in the country 'that neither he or Lord Lansdowne can ever lead the party again to victory'.[56]

Willoughby de Broke's correspondents during this period constantly reiterated the idea that, as the Duke of Bedford argued, 'our stand has saved our party from complete collapse as far as our supporters in the country are concerned.'[57] The Duke of Northumberland suggested keeping the Diehards together to 'put some fight into [Balfour and Lansdowne], & make them feel that if they will not lead us & fight we will fight without them!'[58] Calling for an immediate council of war, Willoughby de Broke told Selborne that they had 'all the men on our side . . . that are worth having. We must keep going.'[59] The Diehards should form a wholly new party — 'a separate organization with its own programme' — or seize control of the old one: 'Most people want a new Party. They simply won't work for Balfour and Lansdowne again. I won't.'[60]

Most of the other prominent ditchers' leaders, including Lords Selborne and Lovat, argued that the 'no-surrender' group should not form a separate party. They agreed, however, that some sort of organisation should be established. Lovat suggested that it would be difficult to hold the Diehards together and proposed instead a more active Opposition Peers Association 'to strengthen the influence which our party could bring on the Front Bench.'[61] Selborne argued that rather than develop a new party, which he believed would be 'impossible to carry out successfully', the Diehards could 'capture the party and Unionist machine lock, stock, and barrel'.[62] These peers agreed that a meeting of the 'No-Surrender group should be called for early October with a view to planning strategy'.[63]

Selborne and other leading Conservative political figures took seriously the threat to foster an organisational split in the party. Selborne kept Austen Chamberlain closely informed as to developments and strove 'to prevent some of our friends from doing anything foolish. There is a movement toward schism, and an atmosphere of intrigue.' He believed that the 'vast majority' of Conservatives agreed with the Diehards.[64] After the first meeting of the 'No-Surrender' group in October, Selborne told Chamberlain that he had acted 'to avoid anything like a split in the party' that might have been created by Willoughby de Broke and his allies.[65] Lord Lovat, concerned that Willoughby de Broke could actually lead a substantial faction away from official Unionist ranks, warned that rather than a separate organisation 'a flexible combine of sorts to stiffen our Party is most advantageous.'[66]

During September and October, Willoughby de Broke, Selborne, Milner, and several Conservatives in the House of Commons, including Austen Chamberlain, Wyndham, Carson, F. E. Smith and Leo Amery, developed plans for a Diehard organisation. Willoughby de Broke invited several Diehard peers and Members of Parliament to attend a meeting on 12 October to formulate a 'militant policy'.[67] By November, Selborne had been elected chairman of a 'Halsbury Club', named after the former Lord Chancellor, and an executive committee, including Willoughby de Broke — in charge of much of the correspondence and organisation — had been selected.[68]

From the first, the Halsbury Club's membership was divided over strategy and goals. These divisions were exemplified by a dispute over the very name of the organisation. According to Salisbury, a minority had favoured the name 'Phoenix' rather than 'Halsbury', to avoid giving offence to those potential supporters who had not favoured opposition to the Parliament Bill. The majority, 'Selborne and his friends', disagreed with this suggestion and also with the notion that the club's action should be confined to influencing public opinion while remaining loyal to the official leaders 'except in extreme cases'. To the majority, including Willoughby de Broke, this course of action was unsatisfactory: 'They were for action in Parliament and they were for forcing the hands of our leaders.'[69] Committees were formed to define a 'forward policy', including a thoroughly reformed but powerful House of Lords, strengthened national defence, social reform and opposition to Home Rule.[70] Considered by the majority of its members to be 'the tip of the party spear', the club attempted to define a programme for which Conservatives would fight and that they could implement for 'the reconstruction of the constitution' after electoral victory.[71]

The official leadership watched the club's activities with interest. Steel-Maitland investigated whether the members intended to unseat Balfour, and reported rather naively that the 'no-surrender principals', including Willoughby de Broke, were 'very anxious to show their loyalty to you'.[72] Other more realistic party leaders feared that the club would perpetuate divisions within the party and that its emphasis on 'fighting spirit' would attract much sympathetic response from Conservatives. Lord Midleton, Secretary of State for War under Balfour, told Curzon that 'unless something is done, three-fourths of the party will drift into the Halsbury Club.'[73] Michael Hicks-Beach, Lord St Aldwyn, told Curzon that the founding of the club was 'proof that the "Die-hard" movement was disloyal on the part of its principal promoters'. In contrast to Midleton, however, St Aldwyn did not believe that 'the strength of this movement goes much beyond the Birmingham gang, and those who are fools enough to be led by Maxse & the *Morning Post*.'[74]

Whatever the numerical strength of the 'Diehard' movement, there can be no doubt that many of its members harassed Balfour in the autumn of 1911 and ultimately helped to drive him from the leadership. In the course of this campaign, close co-ordination developed between a number of prominent peers and Leo Maxse. In September 1911, for example, Maxse announced his intention to introduce a motion 'approving the action of the Die-hards, and thanking them for it' at the next meeting of the National Union. While Selborne denigrated this course of action, fearing that it might breed public dissension and weaken the party, Willoughby de Broke and other leading Diehards, at Maxse's behest, attempted to influence delegates to the Leeds conference in the motion's favour.[75] Lords Leconfield, Stanhope and Bathurst, and the Duke of Somerset, among others, pledged their support and promised to canvass delegates, although Stanhope admitted that he found it 'rather difficult to ask people to go & vote a resolution thanking oneself'.[76] Pressure on the leadership was also applied in other ways. Rowland Prothero, the Duke of Bedford's estate agent, reported that the duke had refused 'to have anything to do with' a scheduled Liberal Unionist conference in Bedford at which Lansdowne was to be the principal speaker, and had forced the meeting to move elsewhere.[77] Lord Scarborough, fearing that the resolution, 'a severe vote of censure on our leaders', might split the party, urged Maxse instead to exert his influence by working to secure the election of a Diehard as chairman of the National Union.[78]

The sniping at Balfour continued as a vigorous campaign in the right-wing press paralleled efforts in Parliament and the Party. On November 8 Balfour resigned. During the struggle for the leadership that followed, Willoughby de Broke and most of the other leading members of the Halsbury Club favoured Austen Chamberlain rather than Walter Long, the representative of the more traditional wing of the party. After the compromise selection of Andrew Bonar Law, Willoughby de Broke wrote to Chamberlain to say, 'how I hoped you would be the leader in the House of Commons'.[79] Willoughby de Broke's support for Chamberlain reflected his faith in the popularity of the tariff-reform programme. Enthusiastic backing for the Chamberlains was thus consistent with Willoughby de Broke's stance throughout the pre-war years. He sought to rouse the electorate and enable Conservatives to reverse the long-standing trend toward Liberalism. His actions during the Irish crisis also reflected these concerns.

Asquith introduced the third Home Rule bill in April 1912 to a Parliament in which the House of Lords could delay legislation for just two years. The Conservative response was to attempt to force a general election during that period and destroy the Liberal government. Once again Willoughby de Broke 'helped to raise the standard of revolt' and, as Lord Curzon recognised, 'ranged at the head of a formidable band' of men who were willing to go to any length to maintain the Union.[80] In March 1912 Willoughby de Broke founded and became chairman of the British League for the Support of Ulster and the Union: 100 peers and 120 Members of Parliament joined immediately. Other leading members included the Duke of Bedford, a leading financier of Conservative causes, Admiral Lord Charles Beresford, a major figure in pre-war naval reform controversies, F. E. Smith, and Ronald McNeill, an Ulster MP and member of the provisional government of Ulster, which Sir Edward Carson had secretly formed during the autumn of 1911.[81] The British League had close connections with Ulstermen who organised and armed the Ulster Volunteer Force, recruiting half-pay and reserve officers to staff the volunteers and helping in gun-running operations.[82]

The British League threatened to lend armed support to Irish Unionists in their effort to thwart Home Rule. Indeed, the League's *raison d'être* lay in the expectation that the Liberal government would call a general election only if convinced of the danger of violent outbreaks. In July 1913, Willoughby de Broke expressed his preference for a general election but warned that 'if that means of settlement is denied to us, then we must fall back on the only other means at our disposal'. He announced in the House of Lords that he and his friends had 'instituted a league', the address of which was 'curiously enough, next door to a gunmaker's shop'.[83] In November, the league publicly appealed to 'men who [had] been trained to bear arms'. By early 1914, it had some 10,000 members.[84]

Throughout 1913, Willoughby de Broke concentrated his energies on the British League. Feeling the need for an alliance with a great national figure who could attract diverse elements and who could be trusted to be as unyielding as himself, he turned to Lord Milner. The former imperial proconsul, whose well-known contempt for parliamentary politics only served to enhance his immense prestige in some Conservative circles, had hitherto remained aloof from the Home Rule struggle. In January 1913, Lord Robert Cecil told Leo Amery, a close ally of Milner and the Chamberlains, that he would not become involved in the more extreme efforts to defeat Home Rule because he would be sorry to see Willoughby de Broke and his 'merry men' inhibited by 'respectable people like Milner and me'.[85] Cecil, however, totally misread Milner's position and tactics. Far from choosing 'respectable' methods of resistance, Milner eventually allied himself fully with the 'merry men'.

The initiative that led to Milner's participation in the Home Rule crisis came from Willoughby de Broke. The generally accepted version of the alliance between Milner and the British League, based on the account of Leo Amery, assigned a passive role to Willoughby de Broke, who supposedly had merely assented on 12 January 1914 to a plan proposed by Amery to Milner on

10 January.[86] In fact, however, Willoughby de Broke had by that date already asked Milner (by letter of 6 January) to join the executive committee of the British League. He explained the league's object, warning that unless force was made ready, the Conservative leadership might 'produce some compromise'.[87] Quickly persuaded, Milner became a leader of the most extreme opponents of Home Rule. He worked on two levels, one public, the other semi-secret. Through Walter Long's Union Defence League and Lord Roberts's League of British Covenanters, Milner organised the drive for signatures to a 'British covenant' pledging resistance to Home Rule. The more secret role of supplying armed force in case of need fell to Willoughby de Broke's British League. It would be the organisation 'to paralyse the Government's action before it reached Ulster', which Milner and Amery had sought.[88] A month after he and Willoughby de Broke had begun working together, Milner told Selborne that the Irish crisis called for action that was 'different, not only in degree, but in kind, from what is appropriate to ordinary political controversies'.[89]

The Home Rule crisis reached its highest peak over the Ulster question. In Belfast, on 28 September 1912, Ulstermen began signing a covenant to defy Home Rule by all necessary means. During 1913 and early 1914, some Ulstermen, including Sir Edward Carson, suggested that a compromise based on the exclusion of Ulster might be acceptable.[90] Members of the British League and many other Unionists angrily rejected this compromise position. Southern Irish landowners recognised that they would be helpless to resist Home Rule if their powerful Ulster allies abandoned the field as the result of a separate arrangement. The Earl of Arran wrote to Willoughby de Broke in October that the Marquess of Londonderry and William Craig would not deny that exclusion had been discussed, despite the fact that Covenanters could not accept such a compromise 'except by breaking their oath which they have taken before their God'.[91] Southern Unionists grew increasingly fearful that the Conservative leadership was 'going to throw over the Unionists in the South & West'.[92] Lord Leconfield, who owned English and Irish land, argued that the leadership would 'give way . . . for certain unless we can stop them'.[93] Many Conservatives who did not own Irish land agreed with him. Ampthill wrote that Willoughby de Broke's fears that 'our leaders may be trapped into some unprincipled and disastrous "compromise"' were shared by all the Conservatives with whom he had worked and that they were glad they could 'count on [Willoughby de Broke] to give us a lead in resistance to anything so fatuous and fatal'.[94]

Willoughby de Broke's opposition to compromise over Ulster did not stem solely from his commitment to the Union. Uppermost in his mind, as always, was the question of the impact of a particular political stance on the Conservative Party and the electorate. As early as December 1910 he and Page Croft had observed in the 'Reveille Manifesto on Home Rule' that 'should the Conservative party abandon its traditional attachment to British institutions . . . it would forfeit the confidence of those to whom it owes its influence and power'.[95] Willoughby de Broke argued that to regain its hold on the electorate, the Unionist Party should reject compromise. The substance of a political position was less important than a show of staunch commitment: 'There is no Party in the State now who can expect to have an overwhelming majority unless they are prepared to take a very strong line about something or another.'[96] Subtle distinctions and niceties of parliamentary debate were worthless in the pursuit of the mass support that alone could bring power. Conservatives must reject an Ulster compromise if they hoped to triumph in the next general election. The average elector 'only understood methods of a more sledgehammer type'.[97]

Willoughby de Broke threw himself into the Ulster crisis in 1914 for a curious combination of reasons; both for the defence of the old order, that is, the traditional Protestant ascendancy, and for what he perceived to be the political requirements of the twentieth century. In early February 1914, just before the opening of Parliament, Willoughby de Broke, Ampthill, Arran, and Stanhope warned their colleagues that Conservative peers might be asked to compromise on the Government of Ireland Bill. They would probably be told that failure to do so would mean that they could be 'chargeable with the bloodguiltiness of Civil War'. The four peers denounced this analysis, arguing that 'the real alternative to Civil War is a Dissolution of Parliament'. To accept the exclusion of Ulster would be to accept the principle of Home Rule; to pass a Home Rule bill before a general election would be to betray a trust.[98] Willoughby de Broke and his allies argued that the Conservatives must move an amendment to the king's speech demanding that the nation 'be consulted' before any form of Home Rule could be considered. The circular met with an enthusiastic response.[99] On 5 February the Conservative front-benchers met at Lansdowne

House and decided to propose such an amendment. Stanhope celebrated this decision as a victory. He wrote to Willoughby de Broke, comparing their efforts to those of an earlier group of Conservative dissidents: 'Whoo-hoop! Really the 4th Party have done pretty well for a first attempt.'[100] Shortly thereafter Lansdowne expressed displeasure that Willoughby de Broke's group had sent out its own 'whip' on 4 February before discovering the opinions of the leadership on the question of an Irish amendment. He noted that the party could have avoided the 'appearance of disunion' if Willoughby de Broke had waited a few hours.[101]

In his speech on the amendment to the address, Willoughby de Broke made the first public suggestion that Conservatives should thwart the Liberal government's power to act in Ireland by amending the Army Annual Act, the measure that provided the legal basis for discipline in the Army. If this act were mutilated, the Army would cease to exist. Willoughby de Broke had discussed this strategy with Maxse at least as early as June 1912.[102] Milner was enthusiastic about the plan, and during early 1914 the party leadership began serious discussions about amending the Annual Act — a committee of the shadow cabinet was appointed for this purpose on 4 February. To the disgust of both Willoughby de Broke and Milner, Bonar Law concluded that most Conservatives would not approve of such subversive activity, and the leadership decided that the Annual Act would be allowed to pass unaltered.[103]

Conservative efforts failed to stop passage of the Government of Ireland Bill for the third time during 1914. In March, seeking to defuse the Ulster issue, Asquith persuaded John Redmond, the nationalist leader, to agree to a compromise plan whereby any Ulster county could choose to be excluded from Home Rule for six years. In May, Asquith announced that an Amending bill providing for the temporary exclusion of Ulster would be introduced. This measure was sent to the Lords on June 23. Most Conservatives detested the bill, and southern Irish landowners rightly regarded it as a grave threat to the unity of the anti-Home Rule forces. The party leadership decided, however, that it should be allowed to pass its second reading and enter the committee stage. Even most of the extreme opposition, including Lord Milner, agreed with this strategy. Willoughby de Broke did not. Despite the pleas of his erstwhile allies, on 1 July he introduced an amendment to reject the bill before the second reading and insisted on a division. His motion was defeated overwhelmingly.[104]

Willoughby de Broke pressed his amendment both as a matter of principle and for tactical reasons. He explained to Halsbury that he believed the bill would solve nothing, that neither Ulstermen nor Nationalists would accept temporary exclusion. He predicted that even if Redmond agreed to the measure — as, in fact, he had done — Redmond would not be able to control his followers in the country, particularly the Nationalist Volunteers.[105] Thus, the bill could not prevent civil war. Willoughby de Broke was not, however, concerned only with Ireland. He declared that if Conservatives agreed to a compromise on Ulster, their party would become a mockery in the country: 'the Party of Home Rule will have reduced the Party of Union to the position of having reduced to writing the terms on which they are prepared to see the Union repealed'.[106] The angry tone and uncompromising stance taken by Willoughby de Broke in his speech on the motion to reject the amending bill prompted the Marquess of Crewe, the Liberal leader in the House of Lords, to pay ironic tribute to him as the 'essence in this House of that spirit which made the passing of the Parliament Act . . . absolutely inevitable if our Parliamentary system was to be preserved at all'.[107]

Impatience with customary English political methods had reached a feverish level in July 1914, and Crewe was surely right that the defeat of Conservative extremists was necessary for the maintenance of traditional parliamentary politics. But the danger did not come simply from those who practised a kind of political obscurantism or who were unable to come to terms with modern political conditions. Much of what Willoughby de Broke stood for was, of course, more characteristic of an earlier age: his appeals for a restoration of paternalist relations between the classes; his celebration of the landed estate; and his sturdy opposition to Home Rule for Ireland. Yet his old-fashioned qualities should not obscure the fact that some of the methods and attitudes that he and like-minded men adopted were anything but traditional.

Willoughby de Broke and his allies sought to utilise the opportunities presented by new political conditions to further staunchly Conservative goals. Often concerned as much with style and appearance as with the substance of politics, Willoughby de Broke argued that the electorate could understand only simple, hard-hitting positions constantly reiterated. He attempted to force his party into adopting such positions and denounced the subtlety, compromise, and qualification that he contended could only confuse the average voter.

In the first year of the Great War, a deeply concerned Lord

Hugh Cecil sensed continuing danger from the Conservative right wing. Warning of the 'great influence' exercised by the section of the Unionist party 'represented by the *Morning Post* and . . . the *National Review*', he noted that 'the whole attitude they adopt toward politics . . . is intolerable . . . and upon two great issues which arise in the future . . . I disagree vehemently with [their] principles . . . I hate Nationalism and I value personal liberty.'[108] Although the style of conservatism represented by Willoughby de Broke and Leo Maxse never gained control of the British Conservative Party, much less of the political life of the nation, it was an important element of pre-war politics. Alarmed by the radical disjuncture between their goals and the realities of English society, Willoughby de Broke and his allies turned to political methods that threatened to undermine political stability and in part anticipated the tactics of later, more successful rightist movements.

Although Willoughby de Broke's political allies gained enormously in power during the first World War, he did not become reconciled to the political establishment. After the war he and other conservatives attacked the reconstruction programme of the Coalition as inadequate. His opposition resulted in part from his study of 'eugenics', the science of race, heredity and environment, which had become popular in political circles. From the 1880s the effects of 'urban degeneration' on national health had been much discussed. After large numbers of recruits for the Boer War were declared unfit, concern mounted among the growing number of those who believed a struggle for world supremacy was inevitable. Social reformers, including the Fabian Society, suggested that the healthier groups in the population should be encouraged and that the 'unfit' should be prevented from multiplying.[109]

Willoughby de Broke found his 'prophet' of racialism in C. W. Saleeby, founder of the Eugenics Society, who argued that all progress and security depended upon the maintenance of the 'quality of the race'. Empires fell because of their very success; once a people no longer had to struggle to survive, natural selection ceased to operate in favour of the most fit. The eugenicist worked to create conditions in which only the best people were allowed to reproduce. Influenced by his close association with the Fabian Society and the National Committee for the Minority Report on the Poor Law, Saleeby convinced Willoughby de Broke that major social reforms were needed to make England stronger.[110]

Willoughby de Broke's concern with the health and strength of

British people prompted him to support women's suffrage, which he believed was 'vital . . . to the general welfare of the nation'. He argued that Parliament had to 'rear such an environment as to bring to maturity the greatest number of healthy men and women'. This great effort would require votes for women in order to obtain 'the effective advice of the mothers of the future race'.[111]

Willoughby de Broke believed that a health ministry should be an important part of a post-war reconstruction programme. The war had convinced him that 'the nation . . . which can bring to maturity the greatest number of healthy men and women . . . will eventually win in the great racial struggle of which this war may only be the beginning.'[112] Much to the irritation of the coalition government, he advocated the immediate establishment of a single institution to supervise health programmes, and angrily deplored the lack of activity in this field of social legislation.[113]

In the years immediately following the Great War, however, decontrol rather than paternalist legislation was in favour. It seemed that the businessmen whom Willoughby de Broke had long distrusted had replaced the older aristocracy and its values. The resolution of the Irish problem and other political events disappointed him. In 1921 he sold his country estate to a manufacturer. At the time of his death he was in the midst of writing his elegiac autobiography *The passing years*, planning to conclude with an appeal to the new owners of the countryside to restore the old relationships between the classes.[114]

Lord Willoughby de Broke died on 16 December 1923 at the age of fifty-four. In a sense it was fitting that he died shortly after the Great War, for in many ways his most striking qualities were characteristic of his social class in the turbulent era which had also come to a close with that struggle. It was a period of confrontation and apocalyptic statements, during which one of his aristocratic allies would state only five months before the War that he was in favour of 'arming and training the classes against the masses.'[115] In Willoughby de Broke could be seen in vivid, primary colours, unmixed with much subtle shading, the concerns of Milner, the Chamberlains, and a large proportion of the landed aristocracy. Confronted with massive social and political change, extreme conservatives reacted fiercely, working to restore the solidity of the mid-Victorian social structure which they recalled from their youth, just as Willoughby de Broke based his politics on the experiences of his childhood and youth on a great Warwickshire estate. The men of the early twentieth century grappled with political and economic problems which steadily eroded their faith in solidity and permanence. External and internal events threatened society as they knew it. Willoughby de Broke strove to uphold traditional values in an age in which they could no longer fulfil the demands of society. Yet his position was not merely an idealisation of the past. He and his political associates understood that adaptations would have to be made to new conditions. But Willoughby de Broke never abandoned his fundamental beliefs about his political and social role and responsibilities. His anxiety about the future, his recognition of serious problems, and his willingness to take extreme steps to solve them, even to the extent of violence, were shared by many of the most important British political figures in the years before the Great War.

Notes

*This chapter is a revised version of an article which appeared in *The Journal of British Studies*, xx, No. 1 (Fall, 1980).

1. George Dangerfield, *The strange death of Liberal England* (Constable, London, 1935), pp. 43–4.
2. Willoughby de Broke, 'The Unionist position', *National Review*, LXII (1913), 213–24. Willoughby de Broke, 'The Tory tradition', *National Review*, LVIII (1911), 208.
3. Lord Willoughby de Broke, *The passing years* (Constable, London, 1924), pp. 2–3, 41–2, 54–5.
4. Ibid., p. 167.
5. The eighteenth Lord Willoughby de Broke to C. A. Hanbury, 9 June 1895, Willoughby de Broke papers (Shakespeare Birthplace Trust, Stratford-upon-Avon), DR 98.
6. Willoughby de Broke (ed.), *The sport of our ancestors* (Constable, London, 1921), pp. 5–6.
7. Willoughby de Broke, *Years*, pp. 148–51. The Earl of Rosslyn, *My gamble with life* (Cassell, London, 1928), p. 4.
8. Willoughby de Broke, *Sport*, pp. 1–2, 17. See also Edward C. Mack, *Public schools and British opinion since 1860* (Methuen, London, 1941) and David Newsome, *Godliness and good learning* (John Murray, London, 1961).
9. Willoughby de Broke to A. Bontwood, 1914, Willoughby de Broke papers, House of Lords Record Office, Hist. Coll. 142, WB 11/2.
10. See, for example, West Sussex Record Office, Lady Bathurst to L. J. Maxse, 8 February 1906, L. J. Maxse Papers, 455, S252; Lord Ebury to L. J. Maxse, 20 July 1906, L. J. Maxse Papers, 456, S328; University of Birmingham Library, L. J. Maxse to Joseph Chamberlain, 23 November 1907, Joseph Chamberlain Papers, JC22/96.
11. See, for example, *Rugby Advertiser*, 16 January 1909, and 19 February 1910; Willoughby de Broke, 'The coming campaign', *National*

Review, LVI (1910), 70.

12. West Sussex Record Office, Willoughby de Broke to L. J. Maxse, 21 March 1909, L. J. Maxse Papers, 459, R64.

13. West Sussex Record Office, Willoughby de Broke to L. J. Maxse, 12 May 1910, L. J. Maxse Papers, 461, R634.

14. Willoughby de Broke, *The passing years*, p. 271.

15. West Sussex Record Office, Willoughby de Broke to L. J. Maxse, 19 June 1910, L. J. Maxse Papers, 461, R664.

16. West Sussex Record Office, Willoughby de Broke to L. J. Maxse, 25 July 1910, L. J. Maxse Papers, 462, R695.

17. West Sussex Record Office, Willoughby de Broke to L. J. Maxse, 20 August 1910, L. J. Maxse Papers, 462, R697.

18. L. J. Maxse, 'Episodes of the month: tapers and tadpoles', *National Review*, LVI (1910), 23.

19. Bodleian Library, Selborne to A. J. Balfour, 24 December 1910, Selborne Papers, 1/40.

20. Bodleian Library, Selborne to Lady Selborne, 21 August 1910, Selborne Papers, 101/94.

21. L. J. Maxse, 'Episodes of the month: "Old Guards" and "Old Gangs": "The Crux"', *National Review*, LVI (1910), 213–14.

22. 'The Unionist reveille', *National Review*, LVI (1910), 367–9.

23. House of Lords Record Office, the Marquess of Lansdowne to Willoughby de Broke, 11 October 1910, Willoughby de Broke Papers, Hist. Coll. 142, WB 1/8.

24. B.L., Willoughby de Broke to the Earl of Halsbury, 10 July 1911, Halsbury Papers, Add. MS 56374, f. 97.

25. Willoughby de Broke, *Years*, p. 289.

26. House of Lords Record Office, George Wyndham to Willoughby de Broke, c. 11 June 1911, Willoughby de Broke Papers, Hist. Coll. 142, WB 2/114.

27. Ibid.

28. See, for example, House of Lords Record Office, Ebury to Willoughby de Broke, 14 June 1911, WB 2/6; Raglan to Willoughby de Broke, 1 June 1911, WB 2/15; Ampthill to Willoughby de Broke, 26 June 1911, WB 2/17. Willoughby de Broke Papers, Hist. Coll. 142.

29. West Sussex Record Office, Willoughby de Broke to L. J. Maxse, 19 June 1911, L. J. Maxse Papers, 463, T84.

30. Ibid.

31. *Parliamentary debates*, Lords, 5th series, vol. 9, col. 931 (9 August 1911).

32. *Parliamentary debates*, Lords, 5th series, vol. 8, cols. 735–6 (23 May 1911).

33. Robert Blake, *The unknown Prime Minister: the life and times of Andrew Bonar Law, 1858–1923* (hereafter, *Unknown*) (Eyre and Spottiswoode, London, 1955), p. 378. Bodleian Library, Lord Milner to Selborne, 19 and 20 July 1911, Selborne Papers, 12/226–33.

34. See, for example, House of Lords Record Office, Rothes to Willoughby de Broke, n.d., WB 2/118; Scarborough to Willoughby de Broke, 27 July 1911, WB 2/42. Willoughby de Broke Papers, Hist. Coll. 142.

35. West Sussex Record Office, Willoughby de Broke to L. J. Maxse, 21 July 1911, L. J. Maxse Papers, 463, T109.
36. On 9 June 1911, Willoughby de Broke had written to Maxse that they should not commit themselves fully to the referendum because it would 'not turn a single vote'. West Sussex Record Office, L. J. Maxse Papers, 463, T85.
37. *Parliamentary debates*, Lords, 5th series, vol. 9, cols. 930-33 (9 August 1911).
38. Bodleian Library, Selborne to Balfour, 24 December 1910, Selborne Papers, 1/143.
39. House of Lords Record Office, Lord Ampthill to Willoughby de Broke, 22 July 1911, Willoughby de Broke Papers, Hist. Coll. 142, WB/2/31.
40. House of Lords Record Office, the Earl of Clarendon to Willoughby de Broke, 31 July 1911, Willoughby de Broke Papers, Hist. Coll. 142, WB 2/63.
41. B.L., the Duke of Somerset to the Earl of Halsbury, 8 May 1911, Halsbury Papers, Add. MS 56374, ff. 83-4.
42. Lord Willoughby de Broke, 'The House of Lords and after', *National Review*, LVII (1911), 395-6.
43. House of Lords Record Office, Lord Stanmore to Willoughby de Broke, 25 July 1911, Willoughby de Broke Papers, Hist. Coll. 142, WB 2/38.
44. *Parliamentary debates*, Lords, 5th series, vol. 7, cols. 28, 777 (6 February and 30 March 1911); *Parliamentary debates*, Lords, 5th series, vol. 8, cols. 799, 883-4 (24 and 25 May 1911); *Parliamentary debates*, Lords, 5th series, vol. 9, cols. 365, 815-32, 858-9, 868-9, 871, 876 (6 July and 8 August 1911).
45. L. J. Maxse, 'Episodes of the month: the noble 500', *National Review*, LV (1910), 710.
46. B.L., L. J. Maxse to J. R. Sandars, 22 July 1911, Balfour Papers, Add. MS 49861, f. 275.
47. West Sussex Record Office, Willoughby de Broke to L. J. Maxse, 21 July 1911, L. J. Maxse Papers, 463, T109.
48. See, for example, House of Lords Record Office, Lord Ampthill to Willoughby de Broke, 13 August 1911, Willoughby de Broke Papers, Hist. Coll. 142, WB 3/25; Wilfrid Scawen Blunt, *My diaries: being a personal narrative of events 1888-1914*, 2 vols. (Alfred A. Knopf, New York, 1921), II, 361.
49. Lord Newton, *Lord Lansdowne: a biography* (Macmillan, London, 1929), p. 424; India Office Library, Lansdowne to Lord Curzon, 25 September 1911; Curzon Papers Eur. F 112/18, f. 92.
50. Liberal Unionist Association, *Memoranda*, New Series, VII, March 1911.
51. L. J. Maxse, 'Episode of the month: leadership', *National Review*, LVI (1911), 717; 'Episode of the month: the leader's understudy', *National Review*, LVI (1911), 905.
52. L. J. Maxse, 'Episodes of the month: tired men', *National Review*, LVII (1911), 573; 'Episodes of the month: Balfourism', *National Review*, LVII (1911), 733.

53. L. J. Maxse, 'Episodes of the month: Foozle folly', *National Review*, LVIII (1911), 11.
54. 'B.M.G.' [L. J. Maxse], 'The Champion Scuttler', *National Review*, LVIII (1911), 215–16.
55. West Sussex Record Office, Willoughby de Broke to L. J. Maxse, 29 January 1911, L. J. Maxse Papers, 463, T9.
56. Bodleian Library, Willoughby de Broke to Selborne, 17 August 1911, Selborne Papers, 74/181–2.
57. House of Lords Record Office, the Duke of Bedford to Willoughby de Broke, 12 August 1911, Willoughby de Broke Papers, Hist. Coll. 142, WB 3/17. Lord Ampthill told Willoughby de Broke, 'We have saved the Unionist Party from utter demoralization.' 13 August 1911, Willoughby de Broke Papers, Hist. Coll. 142, WB 3/25.
58. House of Lords Record Office, the Duke of Northumberland to Willoughby de Broke, 11 August 1911, Willoughby de Broke Papers, Hist. Coll. 142, WB 3/14.
59. Bodleian Library, Willoughby de Broke to Selborne, 12 August 1911, Selborne Papers, 74/176–7.
60. Bodleian Library, Willoughby de Broke to Selborne, 17 August 1911, Selborne Papers, 74/181–2.
61. Lovat proposed that 'all communications between the Opposition Peers Committee and the Front Benches should be via the Opposition Whips . . . that Front Bench men should only attend Opposition Peers meetings by invitation and not by right.' House of Lords Record Office, Lovat to Willoughby de Broke, 17 August 1911, Willoughby de Broke Papers, Hist. Coll. 142, WB 3/44.
62. Bodleian Library, Selborne to George Wyndham, 22 August 1911, Selborne Papers, 74/191. House of Lords Record Office, Selborne to Willoughby de Broke, 18 August 1911, Willoughby de Broke Papers, Hist. Coll. 142, WB 3/46.
63. Bodleian Library, Willoughby de Broke to Selborne, 23 August 1911, Selborne Papers, 74/195–96. House of Lords Record Office, Selborne to Willoughby de Broke, 23, 25 August 1911, Willoughby de Broke Papers, Hist. Coll. 142, WB 3/61, 63.
64. University of Birmingham, Selborne to Austen Chamberlain, 4 September 1911, Austen Chamberlain Papers, AC 9/3/56.
65. University of Birmingham, Selborne to Austen Chamberlain, 7 October 1911, Austen Chamberlain Papers, AC 9/3/57.
66. House of Lords Record Office, Lovat to Willoughby de Broke, 11 October 1911, Willoughby de Broke Papers, Hist. Coll. 142, WB 3/82.
67. B. L., Willoughby de Broke to Halsbury and others, 7 October 1911, Halsbury Papers, Add. MS 56374, f. 200.
68. Bodleian Library, Announcement, 7 November 1911, Selborne Papers, 75/4. B. L., Rules of the Halsbury Club, 17 November 1911, Halsbury Papers, Add. MS 56374, ff. 207–8.
69. B. L., Lord Salisbury to Halsbury, 23 October 1911, Halsbury Papers, Add. MS 56372, ff. 158–60.
70. Austen Chamberlain, *Politics from inside: an epistolary chronicle, 1906–1914* (Cassell, London, 1936), pp. 358–9. L. S. Amery, *My political life*, vol. 1, *England before the storm 1896–1914* (Hutchinson,

London, 1953), p. 411. B. L., Willoughby de Broke to Lord Robert Cecil, 30 November 1911, Cecil of Chelwood Papers, Add. MS 51160, ff. 31–2.

71. University of Birmingham, Selborne to Austen Chamberlain, 7 October 1911, Austen Chamberlain Papers, AC 9/3/57.

72. B. L., A. Steel-Maitland to A. J. Balfour, 17 October 1911, Balfour Papers, Add. MS 49861, ff. 351–5.

73. India Office Library, St John Brodrick to Curzon, 15 October 1911, Curzon Papers, Eur. F. 112/18, ff. 119–20. Chamberlain, *Politics*, p. 371.

74. India Office Library, St Aldwyn to Curzon, 19 October 1911, Curzon Papers Eur. F. 112/18, ff. 1–2.

75. House of Lords Record Office, Selborne to Willoughby de Broke, 5, 12 September 1911, Willoughby de Broke Papers, Hist. Coll. 142, WB 3/67, 69.

76. West Sussex Record Office, Stanhope to L. J. Maxse, 30 October 1911, 464, P839; Leconfield to Maxse, 22 October 1911, 464, P821; Bathurst to Maxse, 30 October 1911, 464, P838; Somerset to Maxse, 11 November 1911, L. J. Maxse Papers, 464, P864.

77. West Sussex Record Office, R. E. Prothero to L. J. Maxse, 28 October 1911, L. J. Maxse Papers, 464, P835.

78. West Sussex Record Office, Scarborough to L. J. Maxse, 31 October 1911, L. J. Maxse Papers, 464, P841.

79. University of Birmingham, Willoughby de Broke to Austen Chamberlain, 12 November 1911, Austen Chamberlain Papers, AC 9/4/9. See also the Earl of Malmesbury to Austen Chamberlain, 11 October 1911, Austen Chamberlain Papers, AC 9/3/4; West Sussex Record Office, Earl Stanhope to L. J. Maxse, 15 November 1911, L. J. Maxse Papers, 464, P859; Blake, *Unknown*, p. 78.

80. *Parliamentary debates*, Lords, 5th series, vol. 6, col. 654 (2 July 1914); *Parliamentary debates*, Lords, 5th series, vol. 42, col. 667 (29 November 1920).

81. National Maritime Museum, T. Comyn Platt to Arnold White, 4 December 1913, Arnold White Papers, WHI/82. Amery, *Life*, vol. 1, p. 414. A. T. Q. Stewart, *The Ulster crisis* (hereafter, *Ulster*) (Faber, London, 1967), pp. 73, 89, 109.

82. Stewart, *Ulster*, pp. 73, 89. 109.

83. *Parliamentary debates*, Lords, 5th series, vol. 14, cols. 921, 924–25 (14 July 1913).

84. Amery, *Life*, vol. 1, p. 440. *Morning Post*, 18 November 1913. Stewart, *Ulster*, pp. 125, 132.

85. Bodleian Library, Lord Robert Cecil to L. S. Amery, 18 January 1913, Milner Add. MSS, 689–10–11–12.

86. Amery, *Life*, vol. 1, pp. 436–7, 440.

87. Bodleian Library, Willoughby de Broke to Milner, 6 January 1914, Milner Add. MSS, 680–2–4.

88. Amery, *Life*, vol. 1, p. 440. A. M. Gollin, *Proconsul in politics: a study of Lord Milner in opposition and in power* (Anthony Blond, New York, 1964), pp. 185–6. Walter Long, *Memories* (Hutchinson, London, 1923), pp. 193–204.

89. Bodleian Library, Milner to Selborne, 18 February 1914, Milner Add. MSS, 689–16–18.

90. P. J. Buckland, *Irish Unionism*, vol. 1, *The Anglo-Irish and the new Ireland, 1885–1922* (Barnes and Noble, New York, 1972), p. 17. Blake, *Unknown*, p. 150.

91. House of Lords Record Office, the Earl of Arran to Willoughby de Broke, 4 October 1913, Willoughby de Broke Papers, Hist. Coll. 142, WB 6/5.

92. House of Lords Record Office, Lord Ashtown to Andrew Bonar Law, 4 May 1914, Andrew Bonar Law Papers, 32/3/8.

93. House of Lords Record Office, Lord Leconfield to Willoughby de Broke, 12 January 1914, Willoughby de Broke Papers, Hist. Coll. 142, WB 7/6.

94. House of Lords Record Office, Ampthill to Willoughby de Broke, 4 January 1914, Willoughby de Broke Papers, Hist. Coll. 142, WB 7/1.

95. L. J. Maxse, 'Episodes of the month: the Reveille Manifesto on Home Rule', *National Review*, LVI (1910), 538–9.

96. *Parliamentary debates*, Lords, 5th series, vol. 15, col. 41 (10 February 1914).

97. Ibid., vol. 15, col. 43 (10 February 1914).

98. House of Lords Record Office, Willoughby de Broke, Arran, Stanhope, and Ampthill to peers, 4 February 1914, Willoughby de Broke Papers, Hist. Coll. 142, WB 8/5.

99. See House of Lords Record Office, Willoughby de Broke Papers, Hist. Coll. 142, WB 8/1–ff.

100. House of Lords Record Office, Stanhope to Willoughby de Broke, 5 February 1914, Willoughby de Broke Papers, Hist. Coll. 142, WB 8/112.

101. House of Lords Record Office, Lansdowne to Willoughby de Broke, 7 February 1914, Willoughby de Broke Papers, Hist. Coll. 142, WB 8/24.

102. West Sussex Record Office, Willoughby de Broke to L. J. Maxse, 16 June 1912, L. J. Maxse Papers, 466, P100.

103. *Parliamentary debates*, Lords, 5th series, vol. 15, col. 39 (10 February 1914); Gollin, *Proconsul*, pp. 187, 207;

104. *Parliamentary debates*, Lords, 5th series, vol. 16, cols. 768–72 (6 July 1914).

105. B. L., Willoughby de Broke to Halsbury, 5 July 1914, Halsbury Papers, Add. MS 56375, ff. 53–4.

106. *Parliamentary debates*, Lords, 5th series, vol. 16, cols. 577–8 (1 July 1914). B. L., Willoughby de Broke to Halsbury, 5 July 1914, Halsbury Papers, Add. MS 56375, ff. 53–4.

107. *Parliamentary debates*, Lords, 5th series, vol. 16, col. 754, (6 July 1914).

108. B. L., Lord Hugh Cecil to Lord Robert Cecil, 10 January 1915, Cecil from Chelwood Papers, Add. MS 51157, ff. 36–7.

109. Gareth Stedman Jones, *Outcast London: a study in the relationship between classes in Victorian society* (Clarendon Press, London, 1971), pp. 308–33. The Earl of Meath, *Memories of the nineteenth century* and *Memories of the twentieth century* (John Murray, London, 1923–4). Arnold White, *Efficiency and empire* (Methuen, London, 1901).

110. Willoughby de Broke to C. W. Saleeby, n.d. (1913–14?),

Willoughby de Broke Papers DR 145/3. Caleb Williams Saleeby, *Biology and history* (Cassell, London, 1908), pp. 5, 8, 11, 12. Samuel Hynes, *The Edwardian turn of mind* (Princeton University Press, Princeton, N.J., 1968), pp. 284–5.

111. *Parliamentary debates*, Lords, 5th series, vol. 16, cols. 83, 89 (6 May 1914).

112. Ibid., vol. 27, col. 507 (10 January 1918).

113. Ibid., vol. 30, cols. 927–32 (17 July 1918); vol. 33, cols. 323–4 (25 February 1919).

114. Willoughby de Broke, *Years*, p. xv.

115. The Duke of Bedford to Willoughby de Broke, 5 March 1914, Willoughby de Broke Papers, Hist. Coll. 142, WB 9/9.

5
George Wyndham: Toryism and Imperialism

J. A. Thompson

George Wyndham is generally cast as a minor Edwardian tragedy. The 'most glittering figure of his age',[1] he collapsed soon after his greatest triumph, the passing of the Irish Land Act of 1903, 'his main practical achievement'.[2] His final years, spent on the opposition front benches, are dismissed as a sad final chapter in a career which ended in 1913 with Wyndham's death at the age of forty-nine.[3]

Wyndham's latest biographer adopts the standard view of his life. Lord Egremont does elaborate on the final phase of Wyndham's career, but not in a way that adds to his reputation. He appears as a strident reactionary whose response to the passing of the Parliament Bill of 1911 exemplified 'the extraordinary hysteria of the moment'[4] shown by landed Tories who clung to a vision of a lost England where contentment 'emanated from the strength of rigidly structured society with firm rural roots.'[5] Wyndham is seen to epitomise the struggle between traditional ideas and the changing social realities of the twentieth century which led to the traumatic crisis of Edwardian England.

Egremont rightly offers Wyndham as a useful political type or symbol. He was hardly a typical landowner, or even a typical Tory Member of Parliament, but he was a typical landed Tory in one respect: he thought and acted in class terms. Egremont goes astray, however, when he claims that Wyndham's world was one of 'blind sentiment, moved by irrational feeling and unfettered by intellectual restraint',[6] and when he implies that Wyndham's position was a mere idealisation of the past. With Wyndham the feeling and reasoning realms were mixed, in a way he himself understood when he wrote, in 1907, 'I despise the French aristocracy for having thrown up the sponge and any man or woman who declines into a praiser of past days.'[7]

In many ways the traditional Tories such as Wyndham were clear-sighted. They were not wrong to conclude that the measures of the Liberal government were something outside the ordinary, that they represented, in the phrase of Lord Rosebery, 'a social and political revolution'. They responded as all classes, under similar circumstances, have responded to the threat of political emasculation. But bitter resistance was not the only response made to the Liberal challenge. Wyndham was prominent among those traditionalists who tried to devise a form of Conservatism which would fulfil the demands of society without changing the traditional basis of English political life.

In his letters Wyndham appears as an artist who drifted into politics, but his family tradition, of which he was acutely conscious, impelled him naturally into Parliament. A family history indicates that the membership of 101 Parliaments between 1439 and 1913 is known. In 57 of these, 38 members of the family sat.[8] Wyndham was convinced that service to the state was a duty of his class. Unlike the French aristocracy, he told Charles Whibley, the gentry of England would not abdicate. It was this obligation which reconciled him to politics.[9]

As Wyndham's father had already discovered, however, family and class obligations, when undertaken in a more democratic age, could conflict with strongly held class prejudices. In 1885, after twenty-five years in the House of Commons, Percy Wyndham surrendered his seat rather than accept an extension of the franchise. And he expressed the wish that his grandson would not do three things:[10]

(1) Become a Roman Catholic;
(2) Marry an American girl;
(3) Go into the House of Commons.

Wyndham himself took (1) and (2) for granted, but it was only later, when he too soured on politics, that he advised his son to shun Parliament and devote himself to a career in the army.

Wyndham was devoted to his parents and they, in turn, were inordinately proud of him. The doting father would silence anyone who was about to interrupt the son's eloquence,[11] and when Wyndham was one of the few prominent Conservatives to retain his seat in 1906, his mother wrote to him:[12]

> I must write for I have been having a succession of splendid omens for you. Well, 1st Splendid Omen of triumphant return at Dover, making me feel and *know* you are in God's hands and you are the man. Thee-*Thou*. Thou art the man who is to redeem your Party Chosen by God and now although it seems like a dream a nightmare that *you alone almost* indeed are absolutely the single Heart and Voice *and soul* to lead your Party thro this first meeting after this burning and Death . . . *Your voice* will be *the* voice to Call forth the new birth — from the Ashes! *Will* be *must be*! May God give you strength to do your best — you must live now like an athlete training for *the* race! and not look to the right hand or the left hand, but *eat drink sleep* and *play* each with the restricted eye of remembrance *of what* you are training for, battle and to meet the Hosts and Hoards — of Philistines — but God will be with you is with you you were born for this.

As Cynthia Asquith observed, the parents adored their brilliant eldest son to the point of idolatry. The son, in return, adopted his parents' view of politics as a series of dramatic battles in which the 'chosen', fighting for the good of England, confronted and routed the 'Philistines'.[13]

Members of Parliament were less indulgent. As a protégé of Arthur Balfour, and as one of the Souls, a distinctive social coterie of the late Victorian upper class whose members played a prominent role in British public life, Wyndham rose effortlessly in politics, but he was never popular in the House of Commons. His 'dandified and over-polished parliamentary manners' irritated Arthur Lee, who quoted an old Tory member as muttering, 'Damn that fellow; he pirouettes like a dancing master.'[14] Lord Crawford thought Wyndham's 'impeccable manners and address' had ruined his career. Later, when describing Anthony Eden, with his 'screen star attitude and moustaches, his mannerisms and faultless costume', he was reminded of Wyndham.[15]

But it was his way of speaking which least pleased the House. Wyndham was eloquent but obscure, original but wordy. In 1898 a sister, Mary Elcho, wrote:[16]

> I think you have a mind that expresses itself very readily in images — the poet's mind with a vivid grasp of the concrete. Your *reasoning* loves to clothe itself in telling hues. You have so many thoughts and so many words, that they almost hustle each other . . . In literature this is a great gift but the danger

in practical conversation is that others *might* think you were *explaining* to them, as if you thought them dull! and that would at once irritate — It is more complimentary to one's audience, though less satisfactory to oneself, to be, almost curtly direct — to fly to the point without preamble, or apology, and without illustration.

Balfour made a similar observation when Austen Chamberlain complained that Wyndham was difficult to understand:[17]

[Wyndham] talks in metaphors. I believe it's his natural way of talking, but it's a great bore for a person with a non-literary mind like mine. I had him for an hour this afternoon, but by dint of cross-questioning him, I think I got out of him what he did mean.

It is striking that Wyndham's only oratorical triumph in the House of Commons came in 1900 with a simple but eloquent address on imperial defence, the dominant theme of his public life.[18]

With Conservative audiences in the country, however, Wyndham became a great favourite, perhaps because he was one of the few contemporary politicians with panache. A picturesque, even splendid figure, he was[19]

Tall, erect, exquisitely attired, with the figure of an Adonis, a head with perfect features, big, bright dark eyes and well-defined dark eye-brows, the whole surmounted by thick wavy silver hair and a well-trimmed moustache of military character.

He stirred crowds, too, with such striking epigrams as 'Listen to the spirit of the Age, but do not forget the Ages', and 'Do not make a scrap-heap of the Past and a treadmill of the Future.' A perceptive friend conceded, however, that Wyndham defended issues in a mode 'too remote and subtle' to make a lasting impression on hearers.[20] He was too uncommon a politician to have profound influence: 'Like most romantics he was moved more by the overall conception of a task, by its significance against the background of history,' than by the details that might be needed to make the vision a reality.[21] Wyndham's speeches, with their picturesque imagery, also gave the impression that he was a sentimentalist. He had not 'the hard sense to do strong things', was the verdict of George Curzon's first wife.[22]

Wyndham's friends believed that his poetic qualities, and his continued attachment to letters, hindered his career. Other politicians distrusted his grace and regarded him as an amateur because he had more than political interests. Others, especially after 1905, thought him indolent and capricious: a grand figure who appeared in the House of Commons only on great occasions and at the best hours.[23] Wyndham certainly was not indolent during his early years in politics. He first made his mark in 1887 as Balfour's industrious private secretary in a Dublin office which issued seventy letters a day. And at the end of the parliamentary session in 1900, when he was under-secretary in the War Office, the *Annual Register* singled him out as a man of 'undoubted ability', although it added that he was too complacent and his speeches were more eloquent than convincing.[24]

It was sustained hard work and heavy drinking while Chief Secretary in Ireland which broke him in 1904, leading to an illness which required some months of rest. Perhaps, as many suggest, he was never the same mentally or physically after his resignation. Certainly he was never the same politically.[25] In late 1904 Edward Stanley wrote, ominously, that Wyndham would never become Balfour's successor: 'he was much too unpopular ever to be leader. He was moreover too fond of the glass.'[26]

The political views Wyndham so distinctly expressed, even in the language of the poet, were rooted in his social position and the imperialism of the late 1880s and the 1890s, the formative years of his political life. His family tradition, representing an idealised past, was infused with an imperial spirit, representing an idealised future, to form his Tory faith.

The Wyndhams were an old English family which had benefited from reformation plunders in south-east England. An early edition of *Burke's Landed Gentry* noted: 'Wyndham, Horner, Popham, and Thynne, When the abbot went out, they came in.' Wyndham's father had purchased an estate of some 3,000 acres near Salisbury in Wiltshire, but as a boy Wyndham spent holidays at Cockermouth Castle, where his mother read to him from Malory's *Morte d'Arthur*. He was so taken with its heroic tales that he insisted on wearing little suits of armour around the house: 'he . . . had the dreams of an Arthurian Knight and doing knightly deeds if they came his way'.[27]

With his own son he read 'Antony and Cleopatra and old books about Cheshire and England, Fuller's "Worthies" and Froissart. For it is our pleasure . . . to retrieve the renown of great men who came from here and fought under the Black Prince.'[28] It is said that Sir Walter Scott was Wyndham's only outpost in the modern world.[29].

Wyndham regarded the gentry, and their way of life, through a reverential haze. A character in a John Galsworthy novel expressed his ancestral mentality perfectly:[30]

> I believe in my father, and his father, and his father's father, the makers and keepers of my estate; and I believe in myself and my son and my son's son. And I believe that we have made the country, and shall keep the country what it is. And I believe in the Public Schools, and especially the Public School that I was at. And I believe in my social equals and the country house, and in things as they are, for ever and ever.

When he was told Liberal budgets would end such a way of life, Wyndham replied:[31]

> even if it should prove to be true, we have no grievance against Fate. We are not forced to say with Fleury, after Sedan, 'Never mind, we have amused ourselves well for twenty years,' because we have been a happy part in the being and doing of England for much longer . . . their [the gentry's] 'urn will not be unlamented.'

It has been said that the significance of a noble family lies in its 'vital memories'.[32] It was his vital memories of the gentry which made Wyndham so sure that the welfare of England rested on its landed elite.

Wyndham held that London was not the proper setting for people of his class: if too much time was spent there it was possible to forget one's true obligations and duties. He criticised those who had begun to look on the country as a place in which to spend only weekends and holidays, and he complained that a friend spent more money on lunches at the Ritz, dinners at Claridge's and suppers at the Carlton than it would cost to keep his country house open for the entire year. The friend thought he was a valuable member of the Conservative Party, but he was undermining the tradition of his class and was helping the radicals to destroy the English land system.[33]

Westminster always remained the centre of Wyndham's ambitions, but he took his duty as a squire seriously. When he succeeded his father in 1911 he outlined ambitious plans for his tenants and for local agriculture. He began a mild 'town-planning' for his native village of Milton in Wiltshire. 'Some people inherit an estate and go on as if nothing had happened,' he wrote. 'I can't do that. I must use all my energy and whatever imagination I may have to get something done that shall last and remain.'[34]

It is not surprising that Wyndham, with his feudal outlook, hated capitalism. It destroyed the old relationship between the classes, which disturbed him; he 'was a real old-fashioned Tory in his devotion to persons, and clung to all that that means in the mutual relations between master and servant, landlord and tenant.'[35] He was eager 'to mete Justice on "the Plutocrats who have bought the Government in order to sell the country"'.[36] 'Cobden's curse' had been fastened on England, at least in part as a result of Robert Peel's betrayal,[37] and it was clear that 'the British Race has one foe — Cosmopolitan Finance with an oriental complexion.'[38] He wrote to Charles Boyd that he had

> twice repaired to the crest of the Cheshire hills and looked at the fat, fair expanse of English fields with their smouldering girdle of chimneys around the far horizon. And I have sworn that they shall not be sucked like eggs by the weasels of pure finance.[39]

Wyndham asked his son, Percy, not to marry an American, a Jewess or an heiress, but rather an English lady.[40] Percy honoured this request and Wyndham was spared the unpleasant spectacle of an enemy in his own family. The three — Americans, Jews and heiresses — summed up for him all the destructive forces at work in the modern age. The road to the Liberal hell was paved with the selfish, irresponsible greed of the capitalists. He rejoiced when the financiers and brewers in his own party were defeated in 1906. It left the field, or so he thought, to those who stood by their names and breeding for a tradition of a thousand years.[41] As for the socialists, they were 'mere mules — without pride of ancestry or hope of posterity'.[42]

Wyndham thought in feudal terms but he recognised that the landed elite must justify its leadership in modern terms. Throughout his political life he spoke the language of the ardent imperialist. He was swept into politics, he informed Joseph Chamberlain in 1903, by a passionately anti-Home-Rule meeting at Her Majesty's theatre in 1886.[43] With the defeat of Home Rule he turned to broader imperial questions. In part to promote the mission of empire, he and other *jeunesse dorée* of the party, 'a clever and over-clever clique of literary Tories',[44] founded the *New Review* in 1894, with W. E. Henley as the nominal editor. When the *Review* failed in 1897 Wyndham almost singlehandedly turned it into *The Outlook and New Review*, later simply *The Outlook*, a weekly journal of foreign affairs, politics and literature which served as a voice for expansionist conservatism.[45]

British imperialist interests were promoted with a brutal frankness. The rights of 'savage nations' were dismissed and 'all means [were] good' in the 'triangular battle between the Anglo-Saxon race, the German race, and the Russian', for the hegemony of the world. Over Fashoda, Wyndham declared,

> We don't care whether the Nile is called English or Egyptian or what it is called, but we mean to have it and we don't mean the French to have it . . . It is not worthwhile drawing distinctions of right and wrong in the matter, it is a matter entirely of interest.

The young Tory imperialists were going in for England's overlordship, Wilfrid Blunt lamented, and they would not stand for any half-measures or economy in pushing it on.[46]

The only part of empire Wyndham visited after taking up politics was South Africa, 'the biggest and most exhilarating thing now going on in the world'. It was there that the English were engaged in a great struggle against 'barbarism and untrained nature'.[47] In Parliament he defended the empire-builders so zealously that for a time he was called the 'Member for South Africa'. He admired Cecil Rhodes, Dr Jameson and Chamberlain, and winked at the cover-up which prevented a parliamentary inquiry from implicating Chamberlain in planning the Jameson raid. Since these men had ventured much, they were forgiven all. Chamberlain was 'the grandest specimen of the courageous, unscrupulous schemer' ever seen in English politics.[48]

Men instinctively took sides for either the Cosmopolitan or the Imperial view, Wyndham believed. And the feeling of the country was, at root, conservative. If the Party played upon the imperial theme, therefore, and offered candidates who loved the past and as imperialists believed in the future, voters would rally to the Conservatives. Had not Dover responded to his populist appeal in 1906?[49]

> All my song has been the brotherhood of the Empire for us

all, fair terms from the Foreigner, and the glory of the Empire for our children — with a little straight talk for Christianity in our schools, as the birthright of English children. I won on Toryism, Empire and Fiscal Reform. The Irish voted for me, the Fishermen voted for me, the Soldiers voted for me, the Artisans voted for me! simply because we liked each other and love the traditions of the past and the Glory of the Future.

When the country failed to respond to the cry 'the empire in danger' in the elections of 1910, Wyndham was shocked, so much so that he repeatedly explained the failure away: The people of England did not realise what was happening.

In 1900 Wyndham predicted that the current wave of patriotism and imperialism would not subside in years, that the opposition had mined itself for a decade, and that the time had come for 'constructive politics' in which, 'Please Heaven', he would have a hand.[50] Later that year he was appointed Chief Secretary for Ireland, a post in which he made and then unmade a great political reputation.

His programme for Ireland was unexceptional but by a happy chance of favourable circumstances his achievement was considerable. Following the policies of his predecessor, Gerald Balfour, Wyndham sought to bring about reconciliation through remedial legislation. What I want, he wrote to his brother in 1901, is 'to smash the agitation, introduce a Land Bill, get money for a Harbour-fishing Policy in the West and float a Catholic University'.[51] He was later accused of flirting with Home Rule, but there is no reason to believe his administration had novel political designs.

Once in Dublin Wyndham's spirits rose when he discovered that Ireland was 'more plastic' than any time since 1887; it had grown weary of 'barren conflict'.[52] The new political atmosphere made possible a Land Purchase Bill acceptable not only to all Irish parties but, by a narrow margin, to a British cabinet increasingly preoccupied with an internal debate over tariff reform. The opposition also supported the measure in Parliament since it advanced a peasant ownership which the Liberals had promoted since 1870.

The Land Act ensured, through financial aid from the state, the voluntary transfer of land from landlord to tenant. A loan to the tenant kept payments below original rents, and a cash bonus to landlords gave them a return over and above the price of holdings.

The purchase price was determined by a Land Commission Court. A massive transfer of land took place under the Act. Within five years 228,938 tenants took possession of their holdings in what John Redmond called 'the most substantial victory gained for centuries by the Irish race for the reconquest of the soil of Ireland by the people'.[53] The political consequences of the Act disappointed Conservatives but the economic ones would have pleased Wyndham. He laid the framework for 'an instinctive parochialism' which dominates Irish society today.[54]

Conservatives spoke of 'killing home rule with kindness': remedial legislation would demonstrate that union with Britain was the best guardian of Irish interests. Early in his term Wyndham declined to speculate on the probable political consequences of his plans, but after the passage of the land act he had a surge of optimism:[55]

> They do believe in me, and tremble towards a belief in the Empire because of their belief in me. By 'they' I mean the whole lot — Unionist, Nationalist, Celt, Norman, Elizabethan, Cromwellian, Williamite, agriculturalist and industrialist, educationalist and folk-lorist. Do not say that I am off again after dreams.

He believed that Ireland could again be moulded to the imperial will if the Irish were given something sensible to think about and work for. In 1912 he was still of the opinion that his land act, if permitted, 'would have made Ireland happy'.[56] The optimism was soon dashed. In 1909 John Dillon told Blunt that ill feeling towards England was stronger than ever in Ireland.[57]

His triumph in 1903 also set Wyndham dreaming of his political future. In June Blunt found him 'romancing almost like a schoolboy' about his career. In September he spoke with his 'usual naive self-confidence' of becoming Prime Minister. He was sure of that. Already, at forty, he was constantly approached about leading the party. His only rival was Curzon, and he was in the House of Lords. Blunt was a sympathetic confidant: Wyndham, he thought, had 'the fire of genius' and was as superior to any English party leader as Disraeli was in his day.[58] Other and more important figures were also impressed: the King expressly asked that Wyndham remain in Ireland, and it was rumoured that Joseph Chamberlain resented his rise to prominence.[59]

The euphoria of 1903 was short-lived. By the spring of 1904

Wyndham was breaking down and, with fatal political consequences, losing his grip on the Irish administration. He was obliged to resign in the spring of 1905 when it was discovered that, despite his denials, he had given unthinking approval to his under-secretary's plans to devolve further powers on the Irish executive. The best defence that could be offered, in itself damning, was that he was unaware of what his colleagues were doing.

Ulster Unionists, never comfortable with Wyndham or his policies, rejoiced at his downfall. Their darkest suspicions were unfounded, but he had not adequately concealed his dislike of their 'sour bigotry' or his personal sympathy for the nationalists. The appointment of a new under-secretary in 1902 had increased their fears. Sir Anthony MacDonnell had great administrative ability but, in working with Unionists, also great handicaps: he was 'an Irishman, a Roman Catholic, and a liberal in politics', with a brother in the Irish nationalist party. MacDonnell had hesitated to accept the post but Wyndham had overridden his reluctance and appointed him with wide freedom of action. The exceptional character of the appointment, when it became known, only confirmed Unionist suspicions: that MacDonnell was 'the mainspring of the Irish administrative machine'. They were reassured only when Walter Long replaced Wyndham and clarified the position of the under-secretary.[60]

The 'devolution crisis' had serious political consequences: it weakened the government of which Wyndham was a member, it undermined moderation and conciliation in Ireland, and it strengthened those who were determined to uphold orthodox unionism. For Wyndham the episode was disastrous to his political reputation, and a halting and ineffective explanation for his resignation, given to the Commons in May, repaired none of the damage. 'I can only thank providence on behalf of yourself and myself that we have no share of the artistic temperament,' Lord Selborne wrote to St John Brodrick after Wyndham's performance.[61] Balfour later said that one of the greatest mistakes of his premiership was letting Wyndham continue in Ireland.[62] And in an otherwise sympathetic essay, E. T. Raymond expressed a common view when he concluded, quoting Galsworthy, that Wyndham was 'too fine and not fine enough'. He was too fine for democratic politics but not fine enough to be indifferent to its prizes or to escape from its vulgarities.[63]

Wyndham never held office again, but he moved to the opposition front benches after Balfour resigned in December 1905. He 'rejoiced' at the opportunity to be himself, which meant, in the wake of the 1906 election, that he began to pull away from Balfour and to ally himself with the most ardent of the tariff reformers. By 1908 he was recognised as a stalwart of their cause. To a limited extent he took an independent line on religious education, defence and social reform.

Wyndham's conversion to tariff reform came belatedly. When Chamberlain launched his campaign in 1903, Wyndham's fighting instincts were aroused: he had not felt 'such exultation in the joy of battle' since 1886. But he declined to join in 'an agitation' on behalf of 'the great question of the future'. Only Chamberlain's imperial message appealed to him and this 'had nothing in common with Protection, and very little with Retaliation'.[63] An uncommitted position appeared, as well, to enhance Wyndham's influence in the Government: in 1903 he seemed to hold the balance of power in the cabinet between the tariff reformers and free traders.

Rather than a single constructive idea, Wyndham advanced a comprehensive programme in 1905 in which he identified his abiding interests:[64]

> I want to save the Party for Imperialism, for Religious Education, for the avoidance of Class conflicts, for the maintenance of the Union (negatively as against constitutional experiments and positively to improve the condition of Ireland and the relations between the 2 countries) and to make Imperial *Defence* at once scientific and economic.

Conspicuously absent from Wyndham's list of party concerns was women's suffrage, although he had spoken in favour of limited enfranchisement in 1892 and 1897. It would, he had predicted, 'sweeten and elevate the atmosphere' of political life in the country.[66] He cast silent votes for an extension of the suffrage in 1908, 1910 and once in 1912, but was absent when the House of Commons divided on the issue in 1904, 1909 and 1911, and a second time in 1912. No reference to votes for women appears in Wyndham's election addresses or printed letters during the Edwardian age.[67]

Wyndham first revealed the passion and some of the rigidity of the Diehard in 1906 when he seized the opportunity to resist the Government's effort to amend the Education Act of 1902 to the disadvantage of Church schools. He insisted that parents had a 'natural and inalienable right' to have denominational instruction in all provided schools. And he argued that religious instruction must be in constant, close and convenient connection with the secular, for religion helped to distinguish man from the brutes and from the machines of the future.[68] He predicted that the issue would develop into 'the most savage fight since the seventeenth century', a 'war to the knife' which he was prepared to wage, 'in front of the line', for five, ten or twenty years.[69] He was bitterly disappointed, therefore, when the Church accepted a compromise in which, as Wyndham saw it, an Anglican archbishop crammed nonconformity down his throat 'with the butt end of his crozier'.[70]

Blunt thought it odd that Wyndham mixed with High-Church people, and championed their cause, when he 'really believes in nothing of these things'.[71] But quite apart from the educational value of the religious stimulus, in which he strongly believed, Wyndham was moved in 1906 by two compelling motives. First, it could be said of him, as it has been said of Balfour, that his motivation was strongly partisan. 'It was his sense of duty towards his party, with its denominational commitments, that fuelled his sustained parliamentary effort.'[72] Some might doubt his soundness on Ireland but none could question the staunchness of his defence of Church interests. Second, the Government's Bill of 1906, if enacted, would have ended the Anglican monopoly of schools in rural areas. In a flight of oratory Wyndham described the fearful social effects of such a change: 'If this Bill passes, rural England will become a howling wilderness, and the solitudes will re-echo nothing but the determined tramp of the rate collector and the harsh commands of the bureaucrat underling.'[73] Liberals mocked Wyndham's rhetoric, but he saw clearly that their legislation would bring to an end the old order in which schools, in the words of Élie Halévy, had been 'built with the squire's money and taught the parson's catechism'.

Although a Conservative spokesman on defence, Wyndham, as an individual, endorsed the aims of the National Service League in June 1909, and again before the League's annual general meeting in June 1911. In February 1910 he was listed as one of the 130 MPs in the new Parliament supporting national service.[74]

Wyndham promoted mandatory training as the only affordable way of giving the country an expeditionary force of 200,000 men, with another 300,000 prepared at every point to take the field for home defence. At a time when Britain faced imperial armies numbered in millions of men, and when the number of bayonets 'talked' in diplomacy as 'money talked' in business, he wrote in 1912, the future of the British Empire turned on 500,000 men in uniform.[75] He readily conceded that national service was not yet 'practical politics' but he expected the NSL to make it so by appealing to 'enlightened patriotism'.

Besides education and defence, 'social reform' was the subject which appeared most frequently in Wyndham's speeches and letters. In 1907 he even threatened to stay out of the next Conservative government unless he was assured it had a definite social policy.[76] On this question he ranged himself firmly on the side of traditional Tory paternalism:[77]

> The State ought to launch the young; and provide a haven for the old. Between youth and age, the State should say that a good man deserves a living. At what year in the human span you can end youth and begin age depends on the amount of wealth accumulated.

But Wyndham's interest never developed beyond the theoretical. Lloyd George kept him and other Tories on the defensive, with even Wyndham complaining in 1912 that the Government was bullying the 'more defenceless' among the poor and insulting the majority of workers over insurance taxes. He was also constrained by his adherence to tariff reform, seen as a precondition to social regeneration. Before the State could tackle the problems of unemployment, sweated labour, housing and the poor law, Wyndham himself wrote, the country must safeguard the home market against state-aided and unjust competition and foster national production. Liberal finance, on the other hand, was a handicap on production and therefore a policy which would only intensify the social evils the Conservatives wished to cure.[78]

Tariff reform, indeed, came to absorb all of Wyndham's political positions. How fully he subscribed to the cause is evident in a letter to his father in 1906:[79]

> Two ideals, and only two, emerge from the vortex: — (1) Imperialism, which demands Unity at Home, between classes, and Unity throughout the Empire; and which *prescribes* Fiscal Reform to secure both. (2) *Insular Socialism* and Class Antagonism. Both these ideals are intellectually reasonable. But the first is based on the past, on experience, and looks to the Future. The second looks only at the Present, through a microscope . . .

As for the 'Liberals' and 'Unionist Free Traders' — the 'Whigs' of our day — Well! Their day is over. It is they who are drowned. The Imperialists and Socialists emerge. That is the dividing line of future parties. The Bankers and Hairdressers and 'épiciers' are out of the hunt.

The first consideration of tariff reform, for Wyndham, was imperial unity and the safety of the country's food supplies. For this reason wheat grown under the flag would be given an advantage, while a duty on foreign wheat would achieve the object of 'victualling this island citadel in time of war'. The revenue gained would be used to finance social reform and lighten the burden of taxes and rates at home. Wyndham summed up his expectations in the peroration of an address he delivered in Liverpool in December 1908: 'The Empire must be defended: the Empire must be united: the manhood of the Empire must be safeguarded.'[80]

As an added appeal, tariff reform promised a state with a frontier. He was staggered to find that the country was becoming a chance part of a cosmopolitan community. In its place, 'He wanted a frontier of consanguinity, not cash. He had a horror of civil and military powers being dictated to by Bankers and Financiers. To clear these rocks he steered quite sincerely, towards an Imperial ring fence.'[81] If tariff reform was primarily a political argument for Chamberlain, it was even more so for Wyndham.

The aggressive tactics of the tariff reformers also had natural appeal for a person of Wyndham's temperament. 'I like troops when I go out to war,' he wrote after a meeting of the Tariff Reform Central Committee in 1912, 'And — I cannot deny it — I like fighting.'[82] Balfour, in contrast, took 'too scientific a view of politics. He knows that there was once an ice age, and that there will some day be an ice age again.'[83] Wyndham made his observation in 1911, but as early as February 1906 he had expressed unhappiness over Balfour's failure to give his followers a clear lead.

Wyndham wrote confidently of the outcome of the struggle between imperialism and socialism — only the first was true and immortal — but in 1909 the Liberals put his faith to the test: they introduced a budget which seemed designed to absorb the socialist ideal while taxing conservative interests and undercutting the appeal of tariff reform. Liberals offered their proposals as 'the first democratic budget', and a triumph of free-trade finance, but Balfour immediately denounced them as 'vindictive, inequitable, based on no principle, and injurious to the productive capacity of the country'.[84] Wyndham stigmatised the Government proposals in similar terms (it was 'the maddest Budget ever introduced') but he welcomed them from the tariff point of view. The budget would make more converts to the cause than any number of speeches.[85]

In the parliamentary struggle over the budget, which consumed 70 days and required 554 divisions, Wyndham took only a minor part. His interventions were few, brief and largely technical in character. But he warmed to the battle as a prominent speaker of the Budget Protest League and he carried the fight against the budget up and down the country during the late summer and autumn. In November he approved of the fighting attitude shown by the peers; they were right to reject the budget and, as Lord Milner advised, to 'damn the consequences'. But such advice meant that Wyndham no longer assumed that his political ideals, or the power of his class, were immortal. He had come to believe, with Lord Rosebery, that Liberal legislation threatened a revolution in which the traditions of the centuries would be destroyed. If this was so, there was no alternative but to fight, with all the weapons available, for survival. Ardent tariff reformers agreed, and their crusade was fought after 1910 'with a determination seen before but infrequently in British politics'.[86]

During the bitter, passionate campaign that followed, Wyndham clung to two convictions: if the Conservatives stood firm, the Government would give way, and in their defiance over the Parliament Bill and Home Rule, the Diehards spoke for the majority of Englishmen. He and his associates lived on the memory of 1886 and the failure of Gladstonian Home Rule. If the Government could be forced to an election or a referendum on the same issue, they believed, the 'English' would rise up against 'the Nationalists' and 'the class forces of separation' and impose imperial consolidation.[87]

To achieve their purpose, however, Conservatives must be men 'firm in heart, and in purpose' who were willing to carry their fight against the enemy 'to the last *extremity.*'[88] If Asquith brought in a Veto Bill (obviously meant to 'suspend' the constitution in order to overcome the nation's 'repugnance' to Home Rule), Wyndham said in February 1911, he should be dared to do his worst: 'You threaten us with a revolution, we threaten you with a counter-revolution . . . we refuse to have the constitution destroyed.' Why should the Conservatives consent to a change in the constitution, Wyndham asked his cousin. They and the king, who would never agree to swamp the House of Lords with new creations, commanded the whole material force of the country besides half of its voting strength. They had the money, the Army, the Navy, the Territorials, even the Boy Scouts.[89]

The Government deserved no consideration, Wyndham wrote in 1912, because it was prepared to sacrifice the care of the State to the instinct of self-preservation:[90]

> Its cohesion depends on pandering to the sectional animosities of its component factions; a sorry business, entailing as it does, the neglect of national interests and, in order that such neglect may escape punishment, the concealment of national perils.

The indictment was harsh but, said Wyndham, to distract the nation at this juncture, by scrapping the Constitution, assailing the Union and despoiling the Church, amounted to 'the political crime of treason'.[91]

Inevitably, as the struggle intensified, bitterness in the political world was reflected in the social. Wyndham declined to join a hunting party with Blunt in December 1910 if Churchill was present. 'But it is impossible for me to denounce my opponents for shattering the Constitution and the Union,' he explained, 'and then, to join with any one of them for the pursuit of pleasure.'[92] Blunt brought the two together again for a weekend in October 1912 but the reunion, as described by his cousin, cannot have given Wyndham satisfaction:[93]

> George Wyndham declared with great oaths that he would rather go to hell than see the British constitution made ridiculous by single chamber Government . . . Winston was very brilliant in all this, as though he kept on at the Madeira he also kept his head, and played with George's wild rushes like a skilled fencer with a greatly superior fence.

Wyndham was less forgiving of old friends who had lobbied for the passage of the Veto Bill. To his wife he wrote on 10 August 1911:[94]

> Of course we can never meet George Curzon or St John Brodrick again, nor can we ever consent to act with Lansdowne or Balfour if they summon Curzon to their

counsels . . . Now we are finished with the cosmopolitan Press — and the American Duchesses — and the Saturday to Mondays at Taplow [Taplow Court, where the Souls often met for weekends] — and all the degrading shams.

Those who voted with the Government, 'against their own convictions', were rats, and even the abstainers had dishonest motives: they were either cowards or, like Curzon, snobs who could not bear to see the prestige of their order diminished.[95]

Immediately after the passing of the Parliament Bill, Wyndham despaired. 'It is a bad business,' he wrote. 'For the moment I cannot see the future.'[96] But he did not retreat to Clouds, his country estate, or into the more congenial world of romantic literature. Instead, he and others, those bound by 'kindred passions for *definite* fighting',[97] formed the Halsbury Club to serve as a permanent ginger group within the Conservative Party. It pledged to restore effective powers to a second chamber, with some, Wyndham included, willing to accept a brand-new house in which peers were elected.[98] To prevent deadlocks between the two chambers, and to avoid the need for frequent elections, Wyndham proposed, 'when the magnitude of the occasion demands it', the use of the referendum.[99] Most Club members supported a full tariff programme, and Wyndham vowed never to accept office in a government which did not give a preference on wheat.[100] In addition, Wyndham informed Austen Chamberlain,[101]

> They wished to speak more plainly about national dangers and National Defence; to give more definite form to the Unionist programme of Social Reform; and in all things to take a more vigorous fighting line . . . They had decided to back Carson for all they were worth in his resistance to Home Rule.

Wyndham was also among those Diehards who vigorously opposed Welsh disestablishment. He did so on Unionist grounds: the party took its stand with the majority of electors in the United Kingdom who believed that religion should be associated with the State.[102]

In his last appearance in the House of Commons, Wyndham supported a private member's bill which called for the introduction of National Service because he was convinced that the voluntary system would not give an adequate territorial force.[103] At the time he was preparing, with L. S. Amery, a scheme of army reform which included a plan for National Service for the Territorials.[104] For Wyndham, as a practical politician, the issue of defence promised multiple rewards: it showed up the inadequate Liberal concern for security, it emphasised the traditional role of the Tories as defenders of the country, and it seemed to offer him, personally, an opportunity to re-establish his standing in the party. Apparently he expected to retrieve, as Minister of War in a Conservative government, the political reputation he had held before the loss of the Irish Secretaryship in 1905. Of course Wyndham's interest in defence went beyond immediate political considerations. Imperial defence was central to his career, as it was, indeed, to the life of his family and class.

Wyndham died suddenly from a blood clot in the heart on 8 June 1913, a little more than a year before the outbreak of the Great War. It was a war he had long expected, and even welcomed as a way of lifting an external threat to the Empire. He would have rejoiced at the upsurge of patriotic sentiment, well expressed by Julian Grenfell, the soldier son of prominent Souls, in a letter sent from South Africa in August 1915:[105]

> It must be wonderful to be in England now: I suppose the excitement is beyond all words . . . It reinforces one's failing belief in the Old Flag and the Mother Country and the Heavy Brigade and the Thin Red Line and the imperial idea which gets rather shadowy in peace time, don't you think?

Wyndham's party and the imperial ideal to which he subscribed benefited enormously from the popular patriotism released in 1914.

Still, fate was undoubtedly kind in the timing of Wyndham's death. Insiders thought that he was slipping, his interventions in parliamentary debates less frequent and less effective. They doubted that he would be in another Conservative government.[106] The war itself drained Wyndham's future — his only child, newly married, died on the western front — and accelerated the decline of the landed interests. Their diminished role was soon confirmed by heavy land sales and rising death duties. In the post-war years, too, the issues of the Diehards — the Empire, the House of Lords, the Irish Union, the Welsh Church and tariff reform — lost either their relevance or their potency. Wyndham was a far less eccentric and a far more significant figure of his own time than historians

George Wyndham

have recognised, but in retrospect it could be said of him, as he said a year after his father's death, 'He would have been unhappy if he had lived.'[107]

Notes

1. The phrase of Max Egremont, in *The cousins: George Wyndham and Wilfrid Scawn Blunt* (Collins, London, 1977), p. 13.
2. *The Dictionary of National Biography: the Concise Dictionary Part II, 1901–1970* (Oxford University Press, London, 1982), p. 742.
3. According to Max Egremont, *Balfour: a life of Arthur James Balfour* (Collins, London, 1980), p. 255, Wyndham died 'exhausted by drink and disappointment'.
4. Ibid., p. 237.
5. Ibid., p. 235.
6. Ibid., p. 112.
7. Guy Wyndham, compiler, *Letters of George Wyndham* (T. and A. Constable, Edinburgh, 1915), II, 223.
8. H. A. Wyndham, *A family history, 1688–1837: the Wyndhams of Somerset, Sussex and Wiltshire* (Oxford University Press, London, 1950), p. 374.
9. J. W. Mackail and Guy Wyndham, *Life and letters of George Wyndham* (Hutchinson, London, n.d.), II, 588.
10. Ibid., p. 586.
11. Cynthia Asquith, *Haply I may remember* (James Barrie, London, 1950), p. 43.
12. Quoted in Nancy Walters Ellenberger, 'The Souls: high society and politics in late Victorian Britain', unpublished Ph.D. dissertation, University of Oregon, 1982, p. 176.
13. Asquith, *Haply I may remember*, p. 43.
14. Alan Clark (ed.), *'A Good Inning': the private papers of Viscount Lee of Fareham* (John Murray, London, 1974), pp. 128–9.
15. John Vincent (ed.), *The Crawford papers: the journals of David Lindsay twenty-seventh Earl of Crawford and tenth Earl of Balcarres, 1871–1940, during the years 1892–1940* (Manchester University Press, Dover, N.H., 1984), p. 606. Perhaps Wyndham was Eden's father. See Robert Rhodes James, *Anthony Eden* (Weidenfeld and Nicolson, London, 1986).
16. Ellenberger, 'The Souls', p. 276.
17. Austen Chamberlain, *Politics from inside* (Yale University Press, New Haven, Conn., 1937), pp. 255–6.
18. *Parliamentary debates*, Commons, Fourth Series, LXXVIII: especially 341–2 (1 February 1900).
19. The description of Lord Croft, *My life of strife* (Hutchinson, London, 1948), p. 73.
20. Charles T. Gatty, *George Wyndham Recognita* (John Murray, London, 1917), pp. 137–8.
21. Egremont, *The cousins*, p. 286.

22. Quoted in Nigel Nicolson, *Mary Curzon* (Harper and Row, New York, 1977), p. 151.

23. In 1911, when reviewing possible successors to Balfour, the party's Chief Whip, David Lindsay, dismissed Wyndham as 'too fussy', 'too flightly' and 'too indolent'. See Vincent, *The Crawford papers*, pp. 237, 297, 314. But Lindsay found most Conservative leaders indolent, and he ignored Wyndham's speaking schedule outside Parliament.

24. The *Annual Register 1900* (Longmans, Green and Co., London, 1901), pp. 62, 180.

25. Of Wyndham's illness and resignation, Nicolas Mosely has written, with a nice touch of the dramatic, 'It was as if the benevolent and amused paternalism of the Souls was cracking . . . and a tougher world was taking over.' Mosely, *Julian Grenfell: his life and the times of his death 1888–1915* (Holt, Rinehart and Winston, New York, 1976), p. 103.

26. Egremont, *Balfour*, p. 191.

27. Shane Leslie, *Men were different* (Michael Joseph, London, 1937), p. 223.

28. Ibid., p. 219. In 1887 Wyndham married Sibell Mary, the widowed daughter-in-law of the Duke of Westminster. They had houses at 35 Park Lane and at Saighton Grange on the Eaton estate in Cheshire.

29. John Biggs-Davison, *George Wyndham: a study in Toryism* (Hodder and Stoughton, London, 1951), p. 236. Scott's appeal, Wyndham explained, was that he 'extracted secrets from oblivion so to endow what is with the charm of what has been . . . He strikes a full chord upon the keys of Time. It is only the greatest musicians of humanity who thus enrich the present by fealty to the past and make it a herald of eternal harmonies.' Mackail and Wyndham, *Life and letters*, II, 581.

30. *The country house* (Heinemann, London, 1948), p. 177. Originally published in 1907.

31. Mackail and Wyndham, *Life and letters*, II, 72.

32. Giuseppe di Lampedusa, *The leopard* (Pantheon, New York, 1960), p. 286.

33. Lord Winterton, *Pre-War* (Macmillan, London, 1932), p. 271.

34. Guy Wyndham, *Letters of George Wyndham*, II, 556.

35. Gatty, *George Wyndham Recognita*, pp. 10–11.

36. Leslie, *Men were different*, p. 224.

37. Biggs-Davidson, *George Wyndham*, pp. 22–3.

38. Mackail and Wyndham, *Life and letters*, II, 602.

39. Ibid.

40. Ibid., p. 739.

41. Egremont, *The cousins*, p. 259. The largest single group in the Conservative Party of the 1906 Parliament has been categorised as 'gentlemen'. See D. J. Dutton, 'The Unionist Party and social policy 1906–1914', *The Historical Journal*, 24, 4 (1981), p. 875.

42. Biggs-Davison, *George Wyndham*, p. 237.

43. Egremont, *The cousins*, p. 24.

44. The description of J. L. Garvin in *The life of Joseph Chamberlain* (Macmillan, London, 1953), vol. 2, pp. 627 and 629.

45. Walter E. Houghton (ed.), *The Wellesley index to Victorian periodicals*

1824–1900 (University of Toronto Press, Toronto, 1979), vol. 3, p. 307.

46. Wilfrid Scawen Blunt, *My diaries, part two, 1900 to 1914* (Martin Secker, London, 1919), pp. 349, 368, 369, 397.

47. Letter to his wife of 8 October 1896, quoted in Ellenberger, 'The Souls', p. 277.

48. Blunt, *My diaries*, p. 346.

49. Mackail and Wyndham, *Life and letters*, II, 537. With a military garrison and a maritime element, and a minority of Nonconformists, Dover had strong Conservative inclinations, however, and returned Conservative members before and after Wyndham's tenure as MP for Dover, 1889–1913. See Henry Pelling, *Social geography of British elections 1885–1910* (St Martin's Press, New York, 1967), p. 76.

50. Letter to Curzon of 17 March 1900, quoted in Ellenberger, 'The Souls', p. 279.

51. Mackail and Wyndham, *Life and letters*, II, 434.

52. Ibid., p. 79.

53. Quoted in Egremont, *The cousins*, p. 236.

54. Andrew Gailey, 'Unionist rhetoric and Irish local government reform, 1895–9', *Irish Historical Studies*, xxiv, No. 93 (May 1984), p. 58, says that Wyndham's Act is one of the few pieces of British legislation to profoundly shape the Irish nation which emerged after 1921.

55. Blunt, *My diaries*, p. 32 and Mackail and Wyndham, *Life and letters*, II, 86.

56. Mackail and Wyndham, II, 720.

57. Blunt, *My diaries*, p. 246.

58. Ibid., pp. 62, 73.

59. Michael Bentley, *Politics without democracy: Great Britain, 1815–1914* (Barnes and Noble, Totowa, N.J., 1985), p. 307.

60. The above discussion is based on F. S. L. Lyons, 'The Irish unionist party and the devolution crisis of 1904–5', *Irish Historical Studies*, vol. VI, no. 21 (1948), pp. 1–22.

61. Egremont, *Balfour*, p. 193.

62. Ibid., p. 194.

63. E. R. Thompson, (E. T. Raymond), *Portraits of the new century* (Doubleday, Doran and Company, New York, 1929), p. 62.

64. Mackail and Wyndham, *Life and letters*, II, 482 and 518.

65. Ibid., p. 501.

66. For his speeches, see *Parliamentary debates*, Commons, Fourth Series, III: 1501–6 (27 April 1892) and XLV: 1216–19 (3 February 1897).

67. If Wyndham did not consider women's suffrage an important question, he was not unlike many other Conservatives. See Constance Rover, *Women's suffrage and party politics in Britain 1866–1914* (Routledge and Kegan Paul, London, 1967), pp. 103–15.

68. See Mackail and Wyndham, II, 545 and *Pariamentary debates*, Fourth Series, CLV: 1068 (9 April 1906) and CLVI: 1027 (7 May 1906).

69. Guy Wyndham, *Letters of George Wyndham*, II, 183–4.

70. Ibid., p. 323.

71. Blunt, *My diaries*, pp. 131, 153. For Wyndham's religious outlook see Gatty, *George Wyndham Recognita*, p. 101, Mosely, *Julian Grenfell*, p. 115 and Robert Speaight, *The life of Hilaire Belloc* (Hollis and Carter,

London, 1957), p. 330.

72. A reference to Balfour's efforts on behalf of the Education Bill of 1902. See Ruddock F. Mackay, *Balfour: intellectual statesman* (Oxford University Press, Oxford, 1985), p. 98.

73. *Parliamentary debates*, Commons, Fourth Series, CLVI: 1029 (7 May 1906).

74. See *The Nation in Arms* for February 1910, August 1911 and Midsummer 1913.

75. Wyndham develops his argument for conscription in the Preface of Lilian Mary Bagge (ed.), *The Unionist Worker's Handbook* (P. S. King and Son, London, 1912).

76. Mackail and Wyndham, II, 594.

77. Ibid., p. 115.

78. Bagge, *The Unionist Worker's Handbook*, p. XVI.

79. Mackail and Wyndham, II, 540.

80. Ibid., p. 115.

81. Gatty, *George Wyndham Recognita*, p. 143.

82. Mackail and Wyndham, II, 721.

83. Blunt, *My diaries*, pp. 131 and 353.

84. Quoted in *The Annual Register 1909*, p. 103.

85. Guy Wyndham, *Letters of George Wyndham*, II, 347 and 348.

86. Richard Jay, *Joseph Chamberlain: a political study* (Oxford University Press, London, 1981), p. 319.

87. Mackail and Wyndham, II, 649.

88. Quoting Napoleon, Mackail and Wyndham, II, 731.

89. Blunt, *My diaries*, p. 371.

90. Bagge, *The Unionist Worker's Handbook*, pp. vii–viii.

91. Ibid., p. xix.

92. Quoted in Egremont, *The cousins*, p. 274.

93. Blunt, *My diaries*, p. 415.

94. Quoted in Egremont, *The cousins*, pp. 278–9 and Ellenberger, 'The Souls', pp. 309–10.

95. Mackail and Wyndham, II, 699. It was said, with nice reverse snobbery, that some voted with the Government because their American wives preferred anything to the diminution of the social value of their titles.

96. Guy Wyndham, *Letters of George Wyndham*, II, 471.

97. Ibid., p. 515. A specific reference to Edward Carson, considered a kindred spirit. Most Conservative MPs, on the other hand, were dismissed as 'shivering sheep-men'.

98. John Barnes and David Nicholson (eds), *The Leo Amery diaries* (Hutchinson, London, 1980), vol. 1, p. 86.

99. See Bagge, *The Unionist Worker's Handbook*, p. xi and *Parliamentary debates*, Commons, Fifth Series: XXI, 2021–2 (22 February 1911).

100. Barnes and Nicholson, *The Leo Amery diaries*, vol. 1, p. 91.

101. Quoted in John Campbell, *F. E. Smith, first Earl of Birkenhead* (Jonathan Cape, London, 1983), p. 248.

102. *Parliamentary debates*, Commons, Fifth Series, XXXVII: 1339–50 (25 April 1912).

103. *Parliamentary debates*, Commons, Fifth Series, LI: 1567–76 (11 April 1913).

104. L. S. Amery, *My political life* (Hutchinson, London, 1953), vol. 2, p. 411.
105. Quoted in Mosely, *Julian Grenfell*, p. 230.
106. See, for example, Arthur Lee in Alan Clark, *'A Good Inning'*, pp. 128-9 and Lord Crawford in John Vincent, *The Crawford papers*, p. 314.
107. Mackail and Wyndham, *Life and letters*, II, 723.

6
Lord Halsbury: Conservatism and Law

Richard A. Cosgrove

The enduring fascination of modern English legal conservatism lies primarily in the various attempts proponents have made to define specifically an unruly and diverse movement. Among the traits conservatives have usually attributed to themselves reverence for the past has played a prominent role. Yet an examination of Edwardian history makes plain some of the fundamental ambiguities that have plagued self-styled conservatives. Perhaps the most basic problem of definition, apart from specific belief, concerns whether Edwardian conservatism consisted of an attitude, a habit of mind, a philosophical vision, or a political programme embodied in the Conservative Party, whose essential purpose demanded success in the political world. For individuals who prized consistency above all else, Edwardian conservatives quarrelled frequently among themselves about how best to characterise their endeavours and follow basic principles. Failure to achieve a consensus made it inevitable that conservatives disagreed on the pressing political and social issues of the day, as in the recriminations over free trade versus tariff reform. The examination of Edwardian conservatism in terms of first principles and political positions becomes essential for an interpretation of Lord Halsbury's public career, in both law and politics. As much as any Edwardian, Halsbury reflected the contradictions of a conservative creed that preached adherence to eternal verities as well as pragmatism in the arena of practical politics.

Edwardian conservatives could not resolve the dilemma of what first principles should act as the primary guide to the formation of a conservative ideology. Lord Hugh Cecil, in the most famous expression of Edwardian conservatism, stipulated in 1912 that

Lord Halsbury

'the recognition of religion implied in establishment and the defence of the endowments against confiscation are essential parts of Conservatism'; and later Cecil added that 'the championship of religion is therefore the most important of the functions of Conservatism'.[1] For some conservatives, therefore, the philosophical principles of conservatism had to reflect a supernatural moral order. Yet other conservatives recognised no such need for religious justification; they deduced a coherent body of principles from secular experience and reposed their trust in this world, not the next.[2] Disagreement on the role religion should play in conservatism represented a basic dispute that contributed to the tone of Edwardian conservatism.

Another important issue, social policy, also indicated the differences that disturbed the desired unity of conservative thought and action. By the advent of the Edwardian age two distinct strains of conservative social policy had evolved. The first component had its roots in a quasi-Disraelian support for traditional paternalism. The rights of property, while sacred, were nevertheless to some extent conditional. Sometimes referred to as the Tory side of conservative policy, this position permitted some acceptance of fledgling Edwardian collectivism. Paternalism and authority preserved the organic society conservatives esteemed against the inroads of urban industrial society.[3] The alternative conservative attitude derived in large measure from Sir Robert Peel's perception that the Conservative Party would survive only by attracting middle-class support.[4] Economic individualism, once denigrated by orthodox conservatives, played an increasing part in the battle against 'socialism' that loomed so large in Edwardian politics. Even this issue was not clear, for tariff reformers wished to introduce protection into a free market economy and aid the beleaguered elements of British industry which no longer competed so successfully in the world economy. Although partisans on either side of the social-policy issue thought of themselves as true conservatives, the principles they cited for support varied significantly.

The relationship between conservative ideology and its political expression, the Conservative Party, also accounted for the confused nature of Edwardian conservatism. The permanence of the party depended in large measure on avoiding reactionary political positions, and its ability, cynical in some cases, to distinguish between its dogmas and the necessities of a given political situation. The tension between principles and tactics became intense in the heated atmosphere of Edwardian politics. The complexities of political factions among conservatives and the Conservative Party have made generalisation difficult: 'There is probably no period in modern English history when official party designations had less application to ideological affiliation than in the immediate prewar years.'[5] Edwardian conservatives suffered from major disagreements about political activities as well as the definition of fundamental principles.

Recent scholarship has emphasised the disparity of action and belief that sheltered within the Conservative Party in the years before the first World War. The various factions included the traditional party organisation identified with Arthur Balfour, the advocates of national efficiency associated with Lord Milner, a segment of radical Tories, generally hostile to the party establishment, who took a lead from the likes of Lord Willoughby de Broke, and those like Leo Maxse who believed that national defence must take priority over all other issues.[6] Of course these groupings were not mutually exclusive, and considerable overlapping added to the confusion on the right. By the beginning of 1911 the Conservative Party had failed to gain office in three successive elections, although its hold on the electorate remained strong. Walter Arnstein has suggested that the Party might well have triumphed in the election of 1915 that the World War precluded.[7] That conservatism possessed major divisions by the time of Sarajevo did not necessarily diminish the electoral appeal of the Conservative Party.

English conservatism, in both ideology and party doctrine, has placed reverence for law among the primary civic virtues, and its regard for the past has frequently led to extravagant praise for the common law as an important element in the superiority of the British Constitution. The common law had survived by its ability to blend stability with change, not as a rigid body of rules. The law had evolved by adherence to precedent while allowing sufficient judicial discretion to keep the common law in touch with altered social conditions. The common law has commanded respect for its vigour, its pragmatic resolution of disputes; legal theory has rarely shaped the contours of the law. The dilemmas of Edwardian conservatism were illustrated by the legal career of Lord Halsbury. To rely on the ancient grandeur of the common law or to stress its adaptability posed a difficulty that troubled many who proudly proclaimed themselves conservatives. The legal dimension of Edwardian conservatism demonstrated the same uncertainties that troubled other areas of conservative policy.

Recognition of the distinctions in conservative thought are particularly apposite in the case of Lord Halsbury. The conventional view of his career as Lord Chancellor aligns him with the radical right faction of the Conservative Party, yet, as Geoffrey Searle has noted, many of the so-called Diehards were impatient with what they termed his ineffective conservatism.[8] Halsbury displayed little interest in the national-defence wing of politics; at one point in 1902 he cancelled his subscription to Leo Maxse's *National Review* because the periodical criticised the Conservative government so bitterly.[9] Halsbury's political career was marked by unwavering loyalty to Conservative Party policies, and Lord Salisbury often consulted Halsbury on political matters while the latter presided on the Woolsack. In his judicial capacity Halsbury appeared in some respects a pillar of legal conservatism, but other aspects of his Lord Chancellorship indicated a willingness to modernise the law and pioneer new areas of legal development. Given the continuous flux of pragmatism and principle in Edwardian conservatism, an examination of Halsbury's career clarifies its legal manifestations.

The most vivid characterisation of Halsbury, and the one by which he remains best remembered, appeared in George Dangerfield's *The strange death of Liberal England*. In the supercharged political atmosphere surrounding the Parliament Act of 1911, the octogenarian Halsbury came to the fore as a symbol of Diehard resistance to the limitation on the power of the House of Lords. In describing Halsbury's unrelenting opposition to the proposed statute Dangerfield wrote: 'Halsbury was a great Englishman, a species of creature which often behaves in a dutiful and disinterested fashion, but is also capable of more eccentricity than all the gentlemen in Europe combined.'[10] It has been unfortunate for Halsbury's reputation that a lifetime of courtroom endeavour, seventeen years as Lord Chancellor, and a long parliamentary career should have taken a back seat to this single episode. Halsbury was surely no backwoodsman, as his extensive political and legal career showed; he was, as Gregory Phillips has written, a 'professional in public service'.[11] He never acquired the trappings of a country gentlman, for he refused to purchase a country retreat and remained a steadfast London resident. The debate on the Parliament Act, with its portrayal of Halsbury as a political neanderthal, made an improper foundation upon which to build an interpretation of a life so varied in achievement.

Hardinge Stanley Giffard was born in 1823, so by the Edwardian period he had already lived a productive life that had witnessed the great changes of the Victorian era. He received his initial education at home under parental tutelage, and as a young man Giffard mastered Greek, Latin and Hebrew; residence near Boulogne also gave him proficiency in French. Despite these substantial linguistic achivements, Giffard took a fourth-class degree at Merton College, Oxford. He apparently paid scant attention to grammatical detail and his examination papers had earned him little regard. After graduation Giffard worked as a journalist for his father's paper, *The Standard*, in London. After preparation at the Inner Temple Giffard was called to the bar in 1850. A relish for the adversarial nature of legal proceedings, combined with a phenomenal memory, gained quick success for the young barrister. Giffard acquired a reputation among solicitors rare for a young man, despite his disconcerting habit of reading his briefs in cavalier fashion. He established a solid though not spectacular practice at the bar, characterised by his careful solicitude for legal procedure.[12]

Among the important cases in which Giffard participated was that of Governor Edward Eyre of Jamaica, for whom he appeared as defence counsel. Legal proceedings against Eyre, which excited public opinion in the late 1860s, stemmed from riots in 1865 in Jamaica. In the suppression of the disorders, Eyre had, by authority of martial law, sanctioned the execution of over 400 blacks, several of whom had been Eyre's severe critics and not connected with the rioting. Successive attempts to make Eyre account for his actions in an English courtroom failed, partly because of Giffard's unhesitating justification of the governor's stern measures. Eventually Giffard succeeded in keeping Eyre free from any legal liability for his actions in the restoration of order. Public interest in the attempts to prosecute Eyre and the failure of Eyre's opponents caused Giffard to regard his role in the affair as 'the greatest triumph of his career at the bar'.[13]

Another case of Giffard's that attracted the interest of the Victorian public became known as that of the Tichborne claimant. This litigation dealt primarily with efforts to authenticate the identity of an individual who had disappeared, was presumed dead, but returned to claim succession to an aristocratic fortune. Giffard initially represented the claimant, but eventually became convinced that his client was not in fact the person he purported to be.[14] The turning-point for Giffard apparently came when the claimant could not recall his alleged mother's Christian name, a lapse in memory that the barrister could not comprehend. Giffard dissociated himself from his client by asking an exorbitant fee to defend him from perjury charges, knowing well that his client could not afford to retain him.[15] Success with governor Eyre and failure with the Tichborne claimant symbolised Giffard's career at the bar, for he, like most leading barristers, knew impressive victory and bitter defeat in equal measure.

In the 1860s Giffard's interests turned towards politics. He joined the National Union of Conservative Associations and developed a forthright political style on public platforms. Participation in major cases added to his political visibility, so in 1868 he stood for Parliament in Cardiff but lost the election by 450 votes. He repeated this attempt in 1874 and again lost, though the margin of defeat in this contest was a bare nine votes. In the Conservative government of 1874 led by Disraeli, Giffard had some claim to political reward, his own lack of success notwithstanding. His contributions to Conservative politics had consisted essentially of providing electoral assistance on platforms to Conservative candidates. He was widely credited with gaining marginal seats for the Conservative cause by virtue of his spirited speeches. Giffard became Solicitor-General in November 1875 after a series of deaths, retirements and political problems had left the Conservative government short of lawyers. With this appointment came a knighthood as well as increased political recognition. In 1877 Giffard secured a seat in the House of Commons at Launceston, enabling him to strengthen the government by his direct political participation.

Giffard did not make a strong impression in the House of Commons. He became increasingly uncomfortable with the new demands of popular politics after 1867. His campaigns had lacked the common touch and his speeches were forensic, not the appealing oratory that most Victorian politicans had mastered.[16] Courtroom style did not necessarily win respect in the rough-and-tumble debates in the Commons. The conservatism he espoused during his tenure as an MP until 1885 derived primarily from party loyalty, not from an independent programme of political positions that he had conceived. Giffard represented the pragmatic side of Conservative politics, eschewing a theoretical philosophy to explain his attitudes. He distrusted many of the changes that affected England, but he was content to express his criticisms within the framework of Conservative Party politics. He spoke infrequently in the House of Commons, yet still acquired a reputation as a keen party man.[17] In 1885, in the new Conservative government led by Lord Salisbury, Giffard accepted the Lord Chancellorship and the accompanying peerage that made him Baron Halsbury. He now embarked at the age of sixty-two upon the judicial career that became his permanent legacy.

If the definition of political conservatism poses many problems, then to provide a useful definition of legal conservatism presents even greater difficulties. In what senses does the term conservative apply to the legal profession? It certainly entails a respect for precedent, yet each party in litigation offers its precedents. Veneration of the past in the form of precedent characterises the entire profession. Even precedent, however, belies this easy definition, because lawyers and courts pay attention to the most recent rulings. A citation to the reign of Henry II simply does not have the same weight as one to the reign of Elizabeth II. If legal conservatism merely means an emphasis on procedural guarantees, every lawyer expects that to characterise a legal system. Opinions may differ about the integrity of a particular legal step, but all lawyers are conservative in their expectation of adherence to formal processes in any legal proceeding. If legal conservatism suggests a reluctance to alter the legal system, then the term implies a futile understanding of the common law itself, for its strength over centuries has rested on its capacity for orderly change that shapes the law to new circumstances. Finally, if 'legal conservative' suggests a person who tries to synthesise the above traits in a professional career then the word 'conservative' loses all meaning, because it encompasses so much that it becomes worthless.

In Anglo-American jurisprudence, fortunately, greater precision is possible when judicial decision-making is involved. Since the middle of the nineteenth century the word 'conservative' has applied to those judges who hold that the judge should find in the various sources of the law the existing basis of law, apply the facts of a case, and then make the appropriate decision. The judge should act as an automaton in an essentially mechanical process. In the course of making his decision the judge must avoid the intrusion of personal beliefs, for the judge should not make new law. The phrase 'judicial restraint' has come to mean contradictory things, but its basic definition warns the judge against the substitution of value judgements for legal decisions. This conception of the judicial process has been defined in many ways, but the most frequent description emphasises its formal nature. Formalism in its simplest expression is a theory of judicial decision-making in which the judge declares the existing state of the law, and permits no other influences in the deductive process.

For the opposition conception of the judicial function jurists have coined the term 'instrumentalism'. In this case the judge chooses among competing interests in the course of litigation and clearly relies upon personal choice in rendering a decision. This definition stresses that judicial activity does involve the making of new law, and makes no apologies for that fact. Instrumentalism emphasises that the judge must consider the consequences of alternative decisions and choose the one that will promote the greatest public welfare. The judge should not regard precedent slavishly, nor should he shrink from changing the law by his decision if circumstances warrant. Thus personal beliefs or public values may influence the hierarchy of legal doctrines according to the preference of the individual jurist. Acknowledgement that a judge utilises personal beliefs in making a judicial decision offends against the view of the ordinary citizen that the legal system should rest upon law, not men. Yet, historically, judicial legislation has constituted the primary vehicle for the adaptability of the common law. Formalism and instrumentalism are not mutually exclusive, and the fascination of judicial analysis lies in the way an individual may embrace one philosophy in certain types of cases while operating differently in other types of cases. The evaluation of Halsbury's Lord Chancellorship and any classification of him as a conservative depends on an understanding of these two analyses of judicial decisions.

Since the Glorious Revolution and the triumph of Parliament, the importance of case law for the study of constitutional history has declined. Before 1688 the Ship Money case, the Five Knights case and others hold a leading place in the unfolding of seventeenth-century events; after 1688 case law arouses little interest in historians. Parliamentary supremacy so exalted the legislature that historians have naturally focused upon statutes as the most important indicator of change. Case law in modern English history has not occupied the central position held by Supreme Court decisions in the United States, where landmark decisions such as *Brown* v. *Board of Education* or *Roe* v. *Wade* addressed crucial issues of American public policy. Few, perhaps only one of Halsbury's decisions, it should be conceded, has had the impact of a major Supreme Court decision. Nevertheless, case law makes the most appropriate test in assessing Lord Halsbury and legal conservatism.

Lord Halsbury

On the surface an interpretation of Halsbury would place him firmly in the formalist camp. He subscribed in public statements to a strict formalist position: 'namely, that English judges merely declared preexisting law'.[18] This position had its roots, ironically, in the Benthamite preference for scientific legislation at the expense of judicial discretion. In 1898, the year in which he was raised to an earldom, Halsbury endorsed a strict theory of precedent in *London Street Tramways Company* v. *London County Council* that, if followed, would have sharply restricted judicial latitude.[19] In addition, Halsbury asserted that judges should interpret statutes in their plain meaning, and not engage in tortuous analysis for the purpose of evading what the statute intended.[20] Halsbury stated his judicial philosophy plainly so that other judges might not deviate from his prescriptions.

Another element of Halsbury's jurisprudence that contributed to his reputation as a legal conservative was his attitude toward academic law. After 1870 the most important movement in Anglo-American legal philosophy emphasised the search for a science of law. Legal study at Oxford and Harvard in particular stressed the necessity to place law on a scientific basis so that it might emulate the intellectual trends of other disciplines. To this imperative Halsbury remained profoundly indifferent, to the great consternation of academic lawyers who put a science of law first on their agenda. Edward Jenks, the legal historian, reported indignantly that to an audience of law students Halsbury had 'cast public ridicule upon the idea of law being taught as a science'.[21] The refusal to embrace the foremost intellectual trend of his later life located Halsbury, according to his critics, firmly in the camp of legal reactionaries. For his part Halsbury had no hesitation in accepting the appellation of conservative, but his long tenure as Lord Chancellor proved more complicated than this simplistic perception.

In Anglo-American constitutional law famous cases become so because they provide judicial guidance in a broad area of public policy. Scholars have commented frequently on the way mundane disputes eventually become test cases for the promulgation of fundamental legal principles. Conversely, issues that have stirred considerable public debate often become decided on narrow constitutional grounds so that an anticipated historic decision does no more than resolve the particular issues at hand without any broader application. Famous cases also produce a peculiar tunnel vision. Because they are usually appellate judgments that address questions of law, not findings of fact, the circumstances that gave rise to the litigation rarely, if ever, make an impression. John Noonan's *Persons and masks of the law* reverses the conventional method of legal analysis by subjecting renowned judges and important cases to a scrutiny of the original events that came to light in the court of first instance.[22] A similar investigation of several of Halsbury's significant decisions demonstrates the ambiguous nature of his legal conservatism. Although he gave intellectual allegiance to formalism, his work on the bench showed a strong instrumental character, mirroring the conflict between pragmatism and principle in Edwardian conservatism in general.

The first example came in the area of martial law, familiar to Halsbury because of his involvement in the Governor Eyre controversy. The legal issue in question focused on the powers conferred in a martial-law situation and the legal consequences that resulted from its imposition. The Boer War supplied the occasions for Halsbury to return to the branch of the law where decades before he had gained his initial reputation. When the Boer War required that military operations be conducted in regions with a hostile population, martial law became the preferred instrument for the maintenance of public order. Since 1628, by virtue of the Petition of Right, whether actual war was raging, as demonstrated by the continued operation of ordinary courts, had served as the criterion for the imposition of martial law. If the civil courts continued in session, then martial law remained unnecessary because the state of disorder did not justify its existence. Between 1628 and the outbreak of the Boer War no occasion had arisen in England that tested this definition. When the case of Mr David F. Marais arose in South Africa owing to the troubled nature of hostilities there, Halsbury seized the opportunity to modernise the ancient doctrines associated with martial law.[23]

Martial law presented Halsbury with an interesting test of his legal and political philosophy. Preferring order to anarchy, as martial law did, posed no major problem, but the idea that individual actions in times of crisis might escape judicial examination or simply disappear under a blanket indemnity was repugnant to traditional ideas of legality. Martial law had caused controversy among seventeenth-century forebears precisely because it conferred fearsome powers on the executive, including authority over life and death. At a time when political conservatism increasingly proclaimed a fear of concentrated government prerogative, the blank cheque extended to government by martial law, regardless of the circumstances, caused some hesitation. The long interval since 1628 guaranteed a modern restatement of martial law, another element presumably against the grain of Halsbury's formalist jurisprudence. The Lord Chancellor did not shrink from the challenge that martial law offered.

On 15 August 1901 David Marais was arrested by the chief constable of Paarl, a township 35 miles from Cape Town, on the instructions of military authorities, for violation of martial-law regulations. The chief constable had no warrant, nor did he even know the cause of Marais's detention. Three days later Marais and other detainees were moved 300 miles to the town of Beaufort West. On 27 August Justice Buchanan presided over a civil court for the district of Paarl because Paarl was undisturbed by the events of war, and civilian courts still exercised uninterrupted jurisdiction. On 12 September Marais, who steadfastly maintained his innocence of wrongdoing, petitioned Justice Buchanan for his freedom on the grounds that his guilt or innocence of any crime should have been adjudicated in the civil court at Paarl. Marais conceded that both Paarl and Beaufort West lay within the districts where martial law existed. In addition, he did not challenge his arrest on the absence of a warrant or his confinement so far from home, for the martial-law regulations of 22 April 1901 specifically granted to the military the authority to arrest without warrant and to send prisoners out of their district. Marais's plea for his liberty was denied by Buchanan because Major-General Wynne submitted an affidavit to the court citing military reasons for the retention of Marais in custody. In view of this assertion Buchanan believed it inappropriate for him to challenge the actions of the military. Marais lost his bid for release but was given leave to appeal.

When the case reached the Judicial Committee of the Privy Council, which heard imperial appeals, Marais was represented by Richard Haldane, the prominent Liberal politician and a future Lord Chancellor in 1912. The primary point of appeal on behalf of Marais rested on the fact that some regular tribunals still operated in the districts placed under martial law. Actual hostilities occurred many miles from Paarl, so the arrest by the authority of the military was illegal. As long as the ordinary courts still operated, the accusations lodged against Marais should have been heard in a civil court. In a famous case from the American Civil War, *ex parte Milligan*, Justice Davis had written with the English precedents in mind: 'Martial law can never exist where the courts are open, and in the proper and unobstructed exercise of their jurisdiction.'[24] Marais's subjection to military authority resulted from an unlawful extension of martial law. The military could assert its authority only when disorder reigned to the extent that the regular courts no longer functioned.

Lord Halsbury rejected the appellant's arguments completely. Halsbury's decision, an 'emphatic statement' as one jurist has written,[25] stressed that the fact that for some purposes a few courts still carried out their usual duties did not constitute conclusive evidence that war was not raging:

> The truth is that no doubt has ever existed that where war actually prevails the ordinary Courts have no jurisdiction over the action of the military authorities . . . Once let the fact of actual war be established, and there is a universal consensus of opinion that the civil Courts have no jurisdiction to call in question the propriety of the action of military authorities.[26]

Halsbury upheld the traditional view that where martial law operated, no civilian court could question the actions of the military. Yet Halsbury also modernised the circumstances that might necessitate the declaration of martial law by taking judicial notice of how warfare itself had changed since the Petition of Right. A definition that had served well since 1628 did not do so in 1901; the passage of time required a restatement of martial law for contemporary conditions.

The application of a formalist-instrumentalist test to the *Marais* judgment is inconclusive. Certainly Halsbury adhered to the precedents that stipulated no civilian control over military actions performed in a martial-law situation. To that extent Halsbury played the role of a formalist who simply took the law as it existed and deduced from the facts at the bar the correct conclusions for the present case. None the less, Halsbury also recognised clearly that changing circumstances required new language and ideas if martial law were to deal effectively with the realities of the South African War. He rejected a rigid interpretation of older authorities in his search for a modern set of legal rules. The *Marais* decision startled many lawyers because it permitted the trial of civilians by military tribunals even while some civil courts remained open.[27] In this sense Halsbury made new law, precisely what he said a judge should not do. Halsbury overruled an 1838 opinion that the military alone could decide whether a situation warranted the proclamation of martial law.[28] The Lord Chancellor held that a civilian court might inquire into the events surrounding martial law, but that once it had been proclaimed, the civilian courts could not interfere with its operation. In a single decision Halsbury combined both old and new law into a modern formulation that was, in effect, new law. In his own mind, however, he had acted in the correct formalist manner.

The difficulty in classifying Halsbury on martial law reflected the dilemmas of conservatism itself in the Edwardian era. Order was preferable to disorder but contemporary life demanded change, and Halsbury recognised the duty to sanction change in order to guide its development. The *Marais* decision left little room for individual rights against military authority, yet Edwardian conservatism sought to promote individualism in the midst of class and party conflict.[29] As Sir Frederick Pollock wrote of Halsbury's logic in *Marais*, an individual who sought *ex post facto* satisfaction for actions taken by military authorities stood little chance of success.[30] Halsbury's language left no possibility of recourse for the ordinary citizen. Harold Laski would later write that Halsbury's work in *Marais* was 'very loose and lacking in that precision of statement which *e.g.* Blackburn or Bowen would have given it'.[31] In his straightforward manner Halsbury believed that the opinion upheld traditional conservative values. Surely individual liberty was among the most important of these, yet was ill-served in this instance. Historian Alice Stopford Green, steadfast Irish partisan and no friend of the Conservative Party, made this critique of Halsbury's Lord Chancellorship: 'The protection of law for the freedom of the citizen in England has been diminished. And that some day many liberties supposed to be secured will have to be recovered. This is the kind of *Nemesis* that comes of the *temper* of outraging principles of law in Ireland & S. Africa.'[32] How to resolve the conflicting claims of the individual and the state troubled Edwardian conservatism, and Halsbury fared no better than other conservatives in trying to frame a consistent policy.

In domestic policy Halsbury's decisions showed a similar ambiguity but, more importantly, they indicated clearly how his personal political opinions could dictate judicial conclusions. In certain areas of public policy Halsbury, the Lord Chancellor who articulated a strict theory of judicial restraint, did not heed his own admonitions. For example, in keeping with prevailing conservative thought Halsbury regarded himself as a true friend of the individual working man, but his judicial career demonstrated a strong aversion to the claims of trade unionism, the corporate expression of that same working man. The solitary worker received his sympathy, but his collective representative roused Halsbury to take extraordinary actions as Lord Chancellor. Proof of his solicitude for the working man appeared in 1900 in *Powell* v. *Main Colliery Co.*, where Halsbury specified that the Workmen's Compensation Act of 1897 should obtain broad interpretation from the courts; that is, judges should not exclude compensation on technicalities but should construe the statute to cover as many cases as possible.[33] The courts should not frustrate the clear intentions of the legislature on this issue. When trade unions were involved in litigation, Halsbury opposed their pretensions with relentless vigour.

Halsbury's most famous case involving unions was *Allen* v. *Flood* where, over his strong dissent, the House of Lords ruled that the tort of conspiracy could not lie against a single trade-union official.[34] By the 1870s a political consensus about the rights of trade unions had united moderate factions in both the Liberal and Conservative Parties, but the law itself still exemplified the individualist bias of earlier decades. At the outset of the Edwardian period the lack of specific legal safeguards did not seem a major problem for trade unions, but Halsbury soon changed that situation. The traditional statutory protections afforded trade unions came under his severe judicial scrutiny and he found them wanting.

The facts of *Allen* v. *Flood* were deceptively simple.[35] William Flood was a union shipwright employed by Glengall Iron Company at Regent Dock in Millwall on a daily basis for ship repair. On 12 April 1894 Flood was employed 'for the job' in the expectation of continued employment on the *Sam Weller* until the overhaul job was completed. In law, however, Flood contracted for one day at a time, so he had no legal right to employment except on a day-by-day basis. On Flood's first day at work some union ironworkers recognised him as someone who had worked as a boilermaker on a previous job. The large boilermakers' union had long attempted to enforce work rules that prevented encroachment by other workers on jobs ironworkers performed. On 13 April Thomas Allen, an official of the Boilermakers' and Ironworkers' Union, visited the shipyard in response to a summons from the local membership. Allen investigated the circumstances, consulted the membership on the job, and then informed the Glengall management that unless Flood was legally dismissed at the end of the work day, the boilermakers would end their employment lawfully and not return to work on the morrow. The company acquiesced in this solution because it feared the disruption inevitable if industrial action occurred upon the retention of Flood.

Flood promptly sued Allen on the grounds that the trade-union official had maliciously interfered with his right to work, and had precluded his right to work for the Glengall Company in the future. In the original testimony witnesses had offered contradictory accounts of whether Allen had threatened that Flood would never work on the Thames again. The court of first instance found in Flood's favour and awarded him damages and costs. The Court of Appeal sustained this verdict but the House of Lords (with Halsbury dissenting strenuously) reversed the judgment and exonerated Allen of wrongdoing. Halsbury offered an extraordinary 23-page dissent, so strongly did he feel that his colleagues had erred in law and policy.[36] The majority held that Allen 'had violated no legal right of the respondent, done no unlawful act, and used no unlawful means in procuring the respondent's dismissal'.[37] Because each party belonged to a union Halsbury had the opportunity to bash the unions without suspicion of bias. In the context of union disagreement he could address the issue of individual versus corporate rights in the workplace.

Halsbury opposed the majority opinion because it undermined the traditional right of an individual to offer labour in the market, which he traced at least as far back as the Glorious Revolution, and which he thought a fundamental constitutional principle. In this case Halsbury imposed a formalist framework on a socio-economic situation he knew little about personally. Although he conceded that the Glengall Company had a legal right to discharge Flood, 'it was Allen who caused the dismissal of the plaintiff'.[38] That Allen should remain responsible for his actions formed the heart of Halsbury's jeremiad; if Flood could not obtain relief, Halsbury believed, the situation infringed all individual liberty. For over a century, however, rules of collective bargaining, with their consequences for employer–employee relations, had evolved without substantial judicial intervention. Halsbury's attempt to repeal history in the name of abstract political principle showed the formalist side of his career that sacrificed reality on the altar of theory. Even here, it should be noted, to hold on to old beliefs in the face of new realities represented a form of instrumentalism in the sense that Halsbury tried to shape the law toward a desired goal.

More controversial was Halsbury's work in the *Taff Vale* decision, a case familiar in general outline to most specialists in the Edwardian period.[39] The right of a union to strike peacefully had existed, most politicians and trade union leaders thought, since the Trade Union Acts of 1871 and 1875. The *Taff Vale* litigation involved a Welsh railway dispute between the Taff Vale Railway Company and the Amalgamated Society of Railway Servants. A strike in August 1900 had generated considerable antagonism because of a personal rivalry between the district manager of the union and the militantly anti-union manager of the railway company. Additionally, the strike had occurred without the approval of the union's general secretary.[40] Initially judgment went against the union on the important issue of whether a trade union was immune from actions for tort, a freedom unions had presumably enjoyed since the 1870s. If union funds became subject to actions for damages incurred in the course of an industrial dispute, all unions had to reconsider a policy of industrial confrontation. Without this legal protection, unions had little opportunity for constructive action.

The *Taff Vale* case quickly made its way through the courts and in July 1901 the House of Lords upheld the original judgment against the union. Halsbury, in a one-paragraph opinion, followed the reasoning of the lower court in accepting that unions were liable for the torts committed by their members.[41] Halsbury added this endorsement:

> If the Legislature has created a thing which can own property, which can employ servants, and which can inflict injury, it must be taken, I think to have impliedly given the power to make it suable in a Court of Law for injuries purposely done by its authority and procurement.[42]

The significant word in that statement was 'impliedly', because it involved Halsbury in the process that he had always criticised, attempting to provide a personal interpretation of legislative intent. His justification was especially suspect because it so neatly put his enemy, the unions, at such a legal disadvantage.

The *Taff Vale* decision, 'the climax of Halsbury's assault on the unions', has persisted as 'one of the politically unhappiest decisions' ever rendered by the House of Lords.[43] The conventional

Lord Halsbury

verdict on *Taff Vale* has held that, whatever the legal merits of the decision, its political consequences were deleterious to the Conservative Party. Halsbury envisaged the common law as ordaining a system of economic individualism; the power of unions to reform that design must be fought at every opportunity. Did *Taff Vale* illustrate a formalist or instrumentalist approach to judicial decision-making? Halsbury relied on an archaic view of industrial relations to reach his decision (formalist), but clearly allowed personal choice to dictate the outcome (instrumentalist). Throughout his career on the bench Halsbury in action exemplified both styles of judicial activity, in concert or individually. A simple description of Halsbury as a legal conservative needs substantial qualification.

Even worse for Halsbury, *Taff Vale* gave to the nascent Labour Party a cause around which to rally, supplying unity to the unions in what they opposed to offset the problems they encountered in formulating a positive programme. Halsbury's role as a Conservative politician could not be separated from his judicial actions, and though few questioned his integrity, *Taff Vale* symbolised a legal decision based on class bitterness. In any event the decision proved futile, for no other damages against unions were ever awarded based on *Taff Vale*. In 1906 the Liberal government, buoyed by its landslide victory, pushed the Trade Disputes Act through Parliament. This not only reversed the *Taff Vale* judgment by providing immunity from tort for unions, but the statute has remained the foundation of trade-union strength for the remainder of the twentieth century. The Conservative opposition in 1906, demoralised by its defeat and afraid to confront the unions, could not summon an effective resistance, and the Trade Disputes Act did not cause a political battle, as did later elements of the Liberal agenda.[44] In the long run, therefore, Halsbury's opposition from the bench to union claims gave to the unions a legal standing they had never previously enjoyed. It brought trade unionists together as no other legal decision did.[45] In the end an unintended consequence triumphed and Halsbury had to endure the hated result.

Another area that bears upon the analysis of Halsbury's legal conservatism was the use the Lord Chancellor made of his patronage powers over appointments to the bench, both to the High Court and to the county courts. His partisanship in the distribution of these positions became something of a public scandal for the manner in which he relied on safe political opinions instead of

Lord Halsbury

legal reputation in the persons he selected. The Lord Chancellorship, a political as well as a legal office, made political soundness an inevitable consideration in the making of appointments. R. F. V. Heuston has challenged the conventional portrait of Halsbury as a Lord Chancellor who populated the judicial system with incompetent ideologues. In nominations to the High Court most of Halsbury's choices proved appropriate, Heuston has argued, and five of them became distinguished judges.[46] Heuston conceded that selections for lower tribunals were not so satisfactory, but the view that Halsbury was motivated only by political considerations did the Lord Chancellor an injustice. Robert Stevens has rejected these conclusions: 'Despite the eloquent and elegant defense by Robert Heuston, there is little doubt that Halsbury appointed judges, both in the appeal courts and at first instance, as much for their political reliability and for political services rendered as for any other reason.'[47] Halsbury doubtless would have regarded the latter assessment as accurate, one for which no apology was needed.

Halsbury's use of political allegiance as one criterion in his judicial appointments reflected the practical side of his official conduct. It might be argued, for example, that a conservative Lord Chancellor ought to approach the law in an ethereal spirit, focusing on the timeless dimensions of the common law. Halsbury rejected this conservative principle in favour of a Conservative policy that made political realities an important element of government. Halsbury typified one conservative strength as expressed by the Conservative Party, the refusal to subordinate practical politics to idealistic visions. Lord Halsbury, the careful guardian of Conservative interests within the judicial system, makes Dangerfield's depiction of a doddering aristocrat ludicrous.

Finally, an aspect of his Lord Chancellorship that shed additional light on Halsbury's perception of his legal role was his willingness to tailor the panel of judges to hear a case in order to achieve a result compatible with his own views. The Lord Chancellor had the undoubted right to assign judges, although the practice usually meant that he would assign a judge to a case in areas of personal expertise. In *Allen* v. *Flood* Halsbury sought to stave off the defeat of his position by summoning additional High Court judges to attend a rehearing in the hope that the enlarged body would reverse the opinion favourable to the unions. The manoeuvre failed, in part apparently because of the resentment Halsbury created by his machinations. In other cases Halsbury delayed the decision in the belief that the majority against him might disintegrate.[48] Halsbury manipulated a flexible system to achieve the results he thought best suited for England. The Lord Chancellor deserved no censure for his actions, for others before and since of different party persuasions have acted in similar fashion. Once again, however, Halsbury acted as a pragmatic lawyer and politician who understood the principles and compromises that had characterised the development of the common law.

Lord Halsbury embodied traditional English conservatism, primarily as a party man who believed Conservative was better than conservative. In its legal manifestation his conservative temper was eminently practical, not some romantic longing for an imaginary past. Halsbury had little time for philosophical musings; he accepted without question that the Conservative Party best represented true conservatism. By the Edwardian era Halsbury was already an old man who believed that he had lived into an age uncongenial to his values. Yet as late as 1916 Halsbury helped out on the bench and the *Laws of England* digest which bears his name were examples of his commitment to useful work. The notoriety Halsbury gained as a radical opponent of the Parliament Act of 1911 should not obscure his lifelong attachment to Conservative politics. His critique of the curtailment of the hereditary principle resulted from his consistent resistance to changes in what he considered fundamental tenets of the constitution.[49] Though theoretically devoted to principle, Halsbury possessed a remarkable flexibility in his judicial activities. The mixture of reverence for the past with a pragmatic accommodation of modernity made Halsbury a conservative who shared the stresses and strains that afflicted Edwardian conservatism. If Halsbury's long career possessed an ambiguity born of principle versus pragmatism, his life reflected the dilemmas that faced all Edwardian conservatives.

Notes

1. Lord Hugh Cecil, *Conservatism* (Thornton Butterworth, London, 1912), pp. 114, 116. A recent restatement of this thesis may be found in William R. Harbour, *The foundations of Conservative thought: an Anglo-American tradition in perspective* (University of Notre Dame Press, Notre Dame, Indiana, 1982), p. 8: 'Religious premises fundamentally shape values central to Conservative political thought.'
2. Reference to this dimension of conservatism is based on the

conclusion by Bob Jessup that English political culture is 'relatively secular in character'. Bob Jessup, *Traditionalism, Conservatism and British political culture* (George Allen and Unwin, London, 1974), p. 24. See also the argument that the 'proper contribution of the conservative spirit, I believe, is to keep alive in human life those ideas and qualities of permanent value which successive generations have accommodated and, more, to make accessible to the present the rich diversity of past experience.' Michael D. Clark, *Coherent variety: the idea of diversity in British and American conservative thought* (Greenwood Press, Westport, Connecticut, 1983), pp. 8-9. Finally, Noël Sullivan concluded that 'English conservatism made little or no attempt to offer the spiritual leadership which Coleridge saw as the only effective antidote to class conflict and the levelling spirit of democratic radicalism.' Noël O'Sullivan, *Conservatism* (J. M. Dent and Sons, London, 1976), p. 89.

3. Harvey Glickman, 'The Toryness of British Conservatism', *Journal of British Studies*, vol. 1, no. 1 (1961), p. 111. See also Philip Norton and Arthur Aughey, *Conservatives and Conservatism* (Temple Smith, London, 1981), p. 285: 'Support for the free market system entails support for private interests and private accumulation of wealth; and such fulsome support for the market economy has never been a dominant feature of Conservative politics.' Finally, see D. J. Dutton, 'The Unionist Party and Social Policy, 1906-1914', *Historical Journal*, vol. 24, no. 4 (1981), p. 872: 'In fact the concept of collectivism is by no means anathema to the mainstream of British Conservatism.'

4. Paul Smith, *Disraelian Conservatism and social reform* (Routledge and Kegan Paul, London, 1967), p. 325; E. J. Feuchtwanger, *Disraeli, democracy and the Tory Party: Conservative leadership and organisation after the Second Reform Bill* (Clarendon Press, Oxford, 1968), p. xiii.

5. Robert J. Scally, *The origins of the Lloyd George Coalition: the politics of social-imperialism, 1900-1918* (Princeton University Press, Princeton, New Jersey, 1975), p. 19.

6. Geoffrey R. Searle, 'Critics of Edwardian society: the case of the radical right' in Alan O'Day (ed.), *The Edwardian age: conflict and stability 1900-1914* (Macmillan, London, 1979), p. 79; Alan Sykes, 'The radical right and the crisis of Conservatism before the first World War', *Historical Journal*, vol. 26, no. 3 (1983), p. 662; and A. J. A. Morris, *The scaremongers: the advocacy of war and rearmament 1896-1914* (Routledge and Kegan Paul, 1984), p. 364.

7. Walter L. Arnstein, 'Edwardian Politics: turbulent spring or Indian summer?' in O'Day, *The Edwardian Age*, p. 78.

8. Geoffrey R. Searle, 'The "revolt from the right" in Edwardian Britain' in Paul Kennedy and Anthony Nicholls (eds), *Nationalist and racialist movements in Britain and Germany before 1914* (Macmillan, London, 1981), p. 29.

9. R. B. McDowell, *British Conservatism* (Faber and Faber, London, 1959), p. 158.

10. George Dangerfield, *The strange death of Liberal England* (Capricorn, New York, 1961), p. 52.

11. Gregory D. Phillips, *The Diehards: aristocratic society and politics in Edwardian England* (Harvard University Press, Cambridge, 1979), p. 12.

Lord Halsbury

12. Alice Wilson Fox, *The Earl of Halsbury: Lord High Chancellor (1823-1921)* (Chapman and Hall, London, 1929), pp. 40-1.
13. Bernard Semmel, *Democracy versus empire: the Jamaican riots of 1865 and the Governor Eyre controversy* (Doubleday, Garden City, New York, 1969), p. 156.
14. Douglas Woodruff, *The Tichborne claimant: a Victorian mystery* (Farrar, Strauss and Cudahy, New York, 1957), p. 251.
15. R. V. F. Heuston, *Lives of the Lord Chancellors 1885-1940* (Clarendon Press, Oxford, 1964), pp. 13-14.
16. Sir Edward Clarke, 1 July 1916, Halsbury papers, quoted in Heuston, *Lives of the Lord Chancellors*, p. 21.
17. Fox, *The Earl of Halsbury*, p. 116.
18. Robert C. Stevens, *Law and Politics: the House of Lords as a judicial body, 1800-1976* (University of North Carolina Press, Chapel Hill, 1978), pp. 89-90.
19. *London Street Tramways* v. *L.C.C.* [1898] A.C. 375.
20. Stevens, *Law and Politics*, p. 90.
21. Edward Jenks to Oliver Wendell Holmes, Jr, 14 August 1900, Holmes papers, Harvard Law School Library.
22. John T. Noonan, *Persons and masks of the Law: Cardozo, Holmes, Jefferson, and Wythe as makers of the masks* (Farrar, Strauss and Giroux, New York, 1976), especially pp. 9-14.
23. *Ex parte Marais* [1902] A.C. 109.
24. *Ex parte Milligan* [1866] 4 Wall. U.S. 2.
25. R. F. V. Heuston, *Essays in constitutional law*, 2nd edn (Oxford University Press, Oxford, 1964), p. 143.
26. *Ex parte Marais* [1902] A.C. 115.
27. Charles Townshend, 'Martial law: legal and administrative problems of civil emergency in Britain and the empire, 1800-1940', *Historical Journal*, vol. 25, no. 1 (1982), p. 182.
28. Heuston, *Essays in constitutional law*, p. 146.
29. Richard A. Cosgrove, 'The Boer War and the modernization of British martial law', *Military Affairs*, vol. 44, no. 3 (1980), pp. 125-6.
30. Sir Frederick Pollock, 'What is martial law?', *Law Quarterly Review*, vol. 18, no. 2 (1902), p. 154.
31. Harold Laski to Holmes, 13 July 1925, in Mark DeWolfe Howe (ed.), *Holmes-Laski letters: the correspondence of Mr Justice Holmes and Harold J. Laski 1916-1935* (2 vols, Harvard University Press, Cambridge, 1953), vol. 1, p. 765.
32. Alice Stopford Green to Holmes, 3 December 1905, Holmes papers. Emphasis in the original.
33. Heuston, *Lives of the Lord Chancellors*, p. 75.
34. *Allen* v. *Flood* [1898] A.C. 1.
35. The best description is in R. V. F. Heuston, 'Judicial prosopography', *Law Quarterly Review*, vol. 102, no. 1 (1986), pp. 94-5.
36. *Allen* v. *Flood* [1898] A.C. 67-90.
37. Heuston, *Lives of the Lord Chancellors*, p. 119.
38. *Allen* v. *Flood* [1898] A.C. 71.
39. *Taff Vale Railway Company* v. *Amalgamated Society of Railway Servants* [1901] A.C. 426.

40. Alice Prochaska, *History of the General Federation of Trade Unions, 1899–1980* (George Allen and Unwin, London, 1982), p. 72.

41. Heuston, *Lives of the Lord Chancellors*, p. 76.

42. *Taff Vale Railway Company* v. *Amalgamated Society of Railway Servants* [1901] A.C. 436.

43. Stevens, *Law and Politics*, pp. 34–5.

44. Opponents of trade unionism, at the time and later, lamented the passage of the Trade Disputes Act. A. V. Dicey wrote in late 1906: 'I am myself firmly convinced that trade unions are attempting to obtain and will obtain an exceptional privilege not possessed by any other person or body of persons.' Dicey to Frederic Maitland, 27 November 1906, Maitland papers, Cambridge University Library. In 1922 James Bryce called the Act 'one of the most unfortunate things done in our time'. Bryce to Dicey, 10 January 1922, Bryce papers, Bodleian Library, Oxford. In addition, see Peter Clarke, 'The Edwardians and the Constitution' in Donald Read (ed.), *Edwardian England* (Croom Helm, London, 1982), p. 43.

45. Keith Laybourn and Jack Reynolds, *Liberalism and the rise of labour* (Croom Helm, London, 1984), pp. 105, 114.

46. Heuston, *Lives of the Lord Chancellors*, p. 65.

47. Stevens, *Law and politics*, pp. 84–5.

48. Ibid., pp. 37–8.

49. Halsbury's opposition fits well into the pattern discerned by Phillips: 'It was a rational and reasoned approach, rather than an emotional reaction based on an unexamined sense of frustration.' Phillips, *The Diehards*, p. 55.

Notes on Contributors

R. J. Q. Adams is a professor of history at the Texas A & M University. He is the author of *Arms and the wizard: Lloyd George and the Ministry of Munitions, 1915–16* (Cassell, London, 1978) and, with Philip P. Poirier, *The conscription controversy in Great Britain, 1900–18* (Macmillan, London, 1987).

Richard A. Cosgrove is an associate professor of history at the University of Arizona. He is the author of *The rule of law: Albert Venn Dicey, Victorian jurist* (Macmillan, London, 1980), and *Our Lady the common law: an Anglo-American legal community, 1870–1930* (New York, New York University Press, 1987).

Arthur Mejia is a professor of history at San Francisco State University. He is the editor, with Gordon Wright, of *An age of controversy* (Harper and Row, New York, 1973), and the co-author of *The modern British monarchy* (St Martin's Press, New York, 1971).

Gregory D. Phillips practises law in Los Angeles, California. He is the author of *The Diehards: aristocratic society and politics in Edwardian England* (Harvard University Press, Cambridge, Mass., 1979).

J. A. Thompson is a professor of history at the University of Kentucky. He is the editor of *The collapse of the British Liberal Party* (D. C. Heath, Lexington, Mass., 1969), and the co-author of *The modern British monarchy* (St Martin's Press, New York, 1971).

Index

Abyssinia 47
Adams, R. J. Q. 41–72
Afghanistan 47–51
Africa 51
  see also South Africa
air force 33–4
Allen, Thomas 142–3
Allen v. *Flood* 142–3, 146
Amery, Leopold 67, 88, 91–2
Ampthill, Lord 83, 92–3
aristocracy 6–7, 79, 106
Army 42, 60, 72
  and Ireland 69–71, 94
  mandatory training 26, 61–9, 117–18
  see also East India Company; Roberts, Field-Marshal Earl
Army Annual Act 94
Arnold-Foster, H. O. 56
Arnstein, Walter 131
Arran, Earl of 92–3
Asquith, Cynthia 107
Asquith, Herbert Henry 13, 28, 63–5, 94

Baldwin, Stanley 25
Balfour, Arthur James 3, 131
  and defence 56–7, 61, 64–5
  and the Parliament Bill 85–7, 121
  and Wyndham 107–9, 115
  opposition to his leadership 78–80, 86–90, 119
Balfour, Gerald 113
Bathurst, Lord 89
Bedford, Duke of 87, 90
Beresford, Admiral Lord Charles 64, 90
Bertie, Lady Gwendoline 15
Bews, Nora (Lady Roberts) 47
Blunt, Wilfred Scawn 112, 114, 117, 121
Boer War 53–6, 60, 138–41

Bonar Law, Andrew 66, 90, 94
Boyd, Charles 111
British League for the Support of Ulster and the Union 90–2
Brodrick, St John 56, 115, 121
Browne, Sir Sam 48
Buchanan, Mr Justice 139
Buller, General Sir Redvers 53–5
Burke, Edmund 16, 20–1, 43
Burma 52

Cambridge, George, Duke of 50, 52
Campbell-Bannerman, Sir Henry 63
capitalism 17
Cardwell, Viscount 50, 60
Carson, Sir Edward 69, 77, 88, 92
case law 136–7
Catholics, emancipation of 16
  see also Ireland
Cavagnari, Major Pierre Louis Napoleon 48
Cecil, Lord David 14
Cecil, Lord Hugh (*later* Lord Quickswood) 5, 11–37
  and air force 33–4
  and Church 23–4
  and coalition government 32–3
  and Ireland 16, 29, 32–3
  and liberty 16, 19, 25–7, 30, 36–7, 95–6
  and marriage 20–3
  and Parliament Bill 13, 19, 24, 28
  and Prayer Book 24–5
  character 13–15, 37
  childhood 11
  philosophy 14–20, 25–6, 30

152

Index

religion 11-13, 16-17, 19-25, 34-5, 129-30
Cecil, Robert Arthur, Marquess of Salisbury (father of Lord Hugh) 3, 11, 52, 132, 135
Cecil, Lord Robert 5, 91
Chamberlain, Austen 25, 33, 36, 77-9, 88-90, 108, 122
Chamberlain, Joseph 5, 18, 27, 111-12, 114, 116, 119
Chamberlain, Neville 25, 77, 79
Chamberlain, Colonel Neville 46
Childers, Erskine 59
Church Assembly 23-4
Church Discipline Bill 23
Churchill, John 15
Churchill, Lord Randolph 51-2
Churchill, Winston 4-5, 15, 21-5, 28-9, 34-6, 121
Clarendon, Earl of 83
Committee of Imperial Defence (CID) 57, 61, 64, 68
Commons, House of 19
conscientious objection 30
conscription 62, 65, 68, 122-3
mandatory military training 26, 61-2, 65-9, 117-18
conservatism 1-2, 58, 129-31
legal 129, 135-6
Constitution of Great Britain 13, 19, 28, 83, 86-7, 120-1, 131
Cosgrove, Richard A. 129-47
Craig, William 92
Cramb, Professor J. A. 67
Crewe, Marquess of 95
Cronje, General Piet 55
Curragh affair 70-1
Curzon, Lord George 80, 85, 89-90, 114, 121-2
Curzon, Lady Mary 108

Dangerfield, George 77, 132, 146
Davis, Mr Justice 139-40
Deceased Wife's Sister's Bill 22
defence 58-69, 123
see also Army
democracy 4, 7
Devlin, Joseph 32

Diehards 5, 80-4, 87-90, 120-2, 132
Dillon, John 114
Disraeli, Benjamin 2-3, 16, 47, 134
'ditchers' 66, 82-7
Dufferin, Lord 52
duty 26, 96-8, 106

East India Company 42-6
Eden, Anthony 25, 107
Education Act (1902) 116-17
Edward, VII, King 114
Egremont, Lord 105
Elcho, Mary 107-8
Elgar, Sir Edward 70
Esher, Lord 56
'eugenics' 96
Eyre, Edward, Governor of Jamaica 133

Fabian Society 96
Flood, William 142-3
France 1, 4, 105-6
French, Sir John 67

Galsworthy, John 110, 115
gentry 97-8, 110
George V, King 66, 82, 84
Germany 59, 64, 68-9
Giffard, Hardinge Stanley *see* Halsbury
Gilbert, Sir William 51
Gladstone, W. E. 2, 11, 52
Gordon, General Charles George 51
Green, Alice Stopford 141
Grenfell, Julian 123

Haldane, Richard Burton 56, 63-5, 67, 139
Halévy, Élie 117
Halifax, Lord 70
Halsbury, Baron, Lord Chancellor (Hardinge Stanley Giffard) 6, 129-47
and conservatism 131-2, 147
and legal science 137
and martial law (*Marais* case) 138-41

Index

and Parliament Bill 66, 81–2, 132, 147
and precedent 136–7
and trade unions 142–5
appointments to the bench 145–6
education and early career 133–5
formalism vs. instrumentalism 135–8, 145
legal conservatism 135–8
Halsbury Club 88–90, 122
Hamilton, General Sir Ian 57, 67
Hayes, Denis 68
health, public 96–7
Henley, W. E. 112
Heuston, R. F. V. 146
Hicks-Beach, Michael 89
Home Rule *see* Ireland
Howard, Michael 65
'Hughligans' 13

ideology 1–4, 6–7
and politics 130–1
imperialism 27, 42, 108, 112–13, 118–19
India 42–6
individual, rights of the 141–3
inequality 18–19, 25–6
'instinct, natural' 20–1
Ireland 6
and Cecil 16, 29, 32–3
and Roberts 53, 69–71, 92
and Willoughby de Broke 90–5
and Wyndham 109, 113–15

Jamaica 133
Jameson, Dr 112
Jenks, Edward 137
justice 18–19, 25
see also Law

Kabul 48–9
Kandahar 49
Kincaid-Smith, Thomas 64
Kipling, Rudyard 52, 70

Land Purchase Act (1903) 6, 113–14

Lansdowne, Marquess of 52–5, 78–80, 85–7, 90, 94, 121
Laski, Harold 141
Law, Andrew Bonar 66, 90, 94
law 6, 131
and public policy 136–7, 141–2
legal conservatism 129, 135–6
martial 48, 138–41
see also Halsbury
League of British Covenanters 92
Leconfield, Lord 89, 92
Lee, Arthur 107
Le Qeux, William 59, 64
Liberal Party
and Ireland 29, 71
and Parliament Bill (*q.v.*) 28
and trade unions 145
and Wolseley 50–1
Lloyd George budget 66, 79, 119–20
liberty 16, 19, 25–7, 30, 36–7, 96
Lloyd-George, David 32–4, 66, 79, 118
Local Government Act (1888) 3
Londonderry, Marquess of 92
Long, Walter 90, 92, 115
Lords, House of 19, 66–7, 81–5
see also Parliament Bill
Lovat, Lord 64, 87–8
Lyttleton, Sir Neville 57
Lytton, Lord 47–8

Macdonnell, Sir Anthony 115
Macmillan, Harold 25
McNeill, Ronald 91
Marais, David F. 138–41
marriage 20–3, 31
martial law 48, 138–41
Maxse, Leo 66, 77, 79–82, 84–7, 89–90, 96, 131–2
Mejia, Arthur, Jr 11–37
Midleton, Lord 89
military training, mandatory 26, 61–9, 117–18
Milner, Lord 70, 77, 82, 88, 91–4, 120, 131

154

Index

Morning Post 86, 89, 96
Mosley, Oswald 12

Namier, Lewis 2
Napier, Sir Robert 47
National Review 77, 79-80, 86-7, 96, 132
National Service League (NSL) 60-8, 117-18
nationalism 19, 27, 30, 96
Newton, Lord 65, 85
Nineteenth Century, The 61-2
Noonan, John 138
North-west Frontier 47-51
Northumberland, Duke of 87

Oliver, F. S. 63
Outlook, The 112

Page Croft, Henry 80, 93
Parliament Bill (1911) 5
  and Cecil 13, 19, 24, 28
  and Halsbury 66, 81-2, 132, 147
  and Roberts 66-7, 70
  and Willoughby de Broke 81-7, 95
  and Wyndham 120-2
patriotism 27, 43, 59, 113, 123
Peel, Sir Robert 2, 16, 130
peers 23, 82-4
  see also Parliament Bill
Petition of Right 138, 140
Phillips, Gregory D. 77-98, 132
Pollock, Sir Frederick 141
Powell v. Main Colliery 142
Prayer Book, revision of 24-5
precedent, legal 136-7
property 17-18, 20, 130
protectionism 18, 27, 79, 116-20, 130
Prothero, Rowland 90

Quickswood, Lord *see* Cecil, Lord Hugh

race 26, 96
Raymond, E. T. 115
Redmond, John 69, 94, 114
referendum 28, 81, 122

reform
  parliamentary 19 (*see* Parliamentary Bill)
  social 18-19, 118-19, 130
  tariff 18, 27, 79, 116-20, 130
religion 2
  Cecil 11-13, 16-17, 19-25, 34-5, 129-30
  Wyndham 116-17, 122
religious education 12-13, 21, 116-17
Rémond, René 1
Repington, Charles à Court 64
'Reveille' group 80, 93
Rhodes, Cecil 54, 112
Richardson, General Sir George 70
Ripon, Lord 49
Roberts, Colonel Abraham 42-5
Roberts, Frederick Sleigh, Field-Marshal, Earl of Kandahar 6, 41-72
  and defence 58-69
  and Ireland 53, 69-71, 92
  and National Service League 60-8
  and Parliament Bill 66-7, 70
  and Wolseley 41, 50-1
  as C.-in-C. 52-7
  childhood and education 43
  health 43, 46, 50
  honours 41-2, 46, 50, 52, 56
  in Afghanistan 47-50
  in India 44-7
  in South Africa 53-6
Roberts, Frederick (son) 47, 54
Rose, Kenneth 11
Roseberry, Earl of 52, 63, 106, 120
Rothermere, Lord 33-4
Royal Air Force 33-4

St. Aldwyn, Lord 89
Saleeby, C. W. 96
Salisbury, Marquess of (Robert Cecil, father of Hugh) 3, 11, 52, 132, 135
Sandhurst 36, 43, 57
Scarborough, Lord 90

Index

Searle, Geoffrey 132
Seeley, J. E. B. 70-1
Selbourne, Earl of 80-3, 87-9, 92, 115
Sepoy mutiny 45-6
Smith, F. E. 70, 88, 91
social reform 18-19, 118-19, 130
socialism 16-18, 111
Somerset, Duke of 83, 90
Souls, the 107, 123
South Africa 36, 53-6, 138-41
Spiers, Edward M. 57
Stanhope, Lord 89-90, 93-4
Stanley, Edward 109
Stanmore, Lord 84
Steel-Maitland, Arthur 85, 89
Steiner, Zara 59
Stevens, Robert 146
Stewart, General Sir Donald 48, 51
suffrage, women's 31-2, 97, 116

Taff Vale case 144-5
tariff reform 18, 27, 79, 116-20, 130
taxation 17, 79, 119
Territorial Force 63-5, 122-3
Tewodros, King of Abyssinia 47
Thibaw, King of Burma 52
Thompson, J. A. 105-24
Tichborne claimant, case of the 133-4
Times, The 13, 25, 64
Tories 2-3
Trade Disputes Act (1906) 145
Trade Union Acts (1871, 1875) 144
trade unions 142-5
Trenchard, Hugh 33-4

Ulster *see* Ireland
Ulster Unionist Party 69-70, 115
Ulster Volunteer Force 70, 91, 95
Union Defence League 92

Verney, Richard Grenville *see* Willoughby de Broke
Victoria, Queen 50, 55-6

Wales, church in 24, 122
Warre, Edmund 79
Weber, Eugene 1
Whigs 2-3
White, Sir George 52, 54
Willoughby de Broke, Baron (Richard Grenville Verney) 6, 77-98
  and eugenics 96-7
  and Halsbury Club 88-90
  and Ireland 90-5
  and Parliament Bill 66, 81-7, 95
  and Party leadership 79-80, 84-90
  and tariff reform 79
  childhood and education 78-9
Wilson, Admiral Sir Arthur 68
Wilson, General Sir Henry 64
Wolseley, Sir Garnet (*later* Field-Marshal Lord) 41, 50-1, 53, 55
women
  enfranchisement of 31-2, 97, 116
  ordination of 34-5
Workmen's Compensation Act (1897) 142
Wyndham, George 6, 105-24, 131
  and Ireland 109, 113-15
  and national defence 117-18, 122-3
  and Parliament Bill 81, 120-2
  and Party leadership 120-2
  and tariff reform 116-20
  character 107-11
  childhood and education 109
  conservatism 105-6
  imperialism 108, 112-13, 123
  parents 106-7
  religion 116-17, 122
Wyndham, Percy (father of George) 106
Wyndham, Percy (son of George) 106, 111, 123
Wynne, Major-General 139